NEVER TOO OLD

Life lessons from a second-career missionary in Kenya

By

Ruth Henningham

Grosvenor House
Publishing Limited

This book is published by
Grosvenor House Publishing Ltd
Link House
140 The Broadway, Tolworth, Surrey, KT6 7HT.
www.grosvenorhousepublishing.co.uk

A CIP record for this book
is available from the British Library

Paperback ISBN 978-1-83615-251-4
eBook ISBN 978-1-83615-252-1

To my children who encouraged me
in my new venture in Kenya

Nikki
Deb
David

Thanks to
Rosemary Heden
John Harris
Janine Harris

for their diligence in reading and
correcting my writing

Contents

Foreword

Have you ever wondered whether you're too old to learn new things? Too old to learn from the Lord? Do you ever wonder where your life is going? If so, you've picked up the right book!

Over the next few pages, you will join Ruth on her journey of spiritual experience and understanding as she works through the Lord's plans for her and what it really means to never be too old to learn. Contained within the story are moments of danger, humour, sadness and hope, as we walk with Ruth through the extraordinary ups and downs of a sudden change in the direction of her life at the age of 60. Through it all Ruth helps her readers see more of God's hand at work in her life, sharing with us all the things she learns along the way.

I loved reading Ruth's story because despite knowing Ruth and being aware of parts of her story before, I never knew all the extraordinary details that are contained in this book. I loved reading of her adventures, of the people she met and particularly her descriptions of Kenya. I love how she is so realistic; at no point in reading do you think that Ruth is simply a superwoman and does all the amazing things she does in her own strength. Instead, I spent the entire book on the edge of my seat wondering not 'what will Ruth do next?' but 'what will God do next?' Because while this is a story about Ruth, more than anything it is a story about God. This is the story of a God who never gives up on His people, who always has plans for them and whose plans are always bigger and better than ours. It is a story that will surprise you and one that will encourage you, I do hope you enjoy going on that adventure of discovery with Ruth as much as I did.

Emily Agnew

1. Learning to Listen to the Lord

1.1 Where is my life going?

For I know the plans I have for you," declares the Lord,
"plans to prosper you and not to harm you,
plans to give you hope and a future.
Jeremiah 29:11 NIV

I looked out of the window, it was pitch dark outside. The flight had been long and uneventful but that was about to change. We had been served our breakfast and an announcement from the captain was loud and clear, "We will soon be coming into land at Nairobi airport but the airport is shut down because of serious rioting in the city and your friends may not be there to meet you, so you must be prepared to stay in the airport for the night."

Kenya had just had elections and the violence was in protest over the results. The Kenyan woman in the seat next to me grabbed my hand and pleaded with me, "Please stay with me, I am so frightened." I told her I would. She was hoping to transfer to a flight for Mombasa but we had no idea what to expect. As we disembarked from the aeroplane she was directed along the route for transfers so we lost touch at that point.

How did I come to be here in these circumstances?

I was a widow from the UK, aged 60, and my circumstances and the Lord's plans for me had brought me to this point and I would like to share my journey of spiritual experience and understanding with you.

My husband John had been diagnosed with terminal cancer and after several years of treatment, we had decided to spend whatever time he had left together. So, with only another two years until retirement, I took it early and left my job as a primary school teacher.

Facing the impending loss of my husband was no easy matter, but over the years of his illness we had been learning how to lean on the Lord and trust him daily. We prayed that God would heal John but, when the answer was an obvious no, I heard him say, "Well if I am not going to be healed, then please show me what you want me to do with the time I have left." Every day from then on he asked the Lord to bring someone to him that he could share his faith and hope with. In the hospital, to our great surprise, he became known among the doctors as "that man of great faith".

John was becoming more and more concerned for me and wanted me to establish a routine that would continue when he had gone, to minimise, in his eyes, the feeling of loss. We had a strong church family who were very supportive. Interlaced with hospital visits, I worked among the women's bible study group, started a bible theology study course, made leaflets for Sunday school and helped another friend who was also facing terminal cancer.

John had an amazing doctor who was determined to keep him alive for as long as he could. John was once again taken into hospital for surgery and on one visit he began to talk again of things I needed to do to make life easier for me when he was no longer there. I found these conversations very distressing but I didn't want to upset him, so we continued to talk. After the visit I had a two hour journey to get home on public transport. Near to tears, I boarded the train and just prayed that the Lord would get me home as quickly as possible. As the train approached the station for my next connection, the loudspeaker announced that the train was not going any further because of a riot at the next station and we would have to find alternative routes. This was disastrous, as my journey would now take much longer. I made my way to another platform and took a train that would deliver me to the far side of my home town instead of to the end of my street. I left the train and went to find a bus to complete the journey, feeling more depressed than ever. I boarded the bus and sat down in the nearest empty seat and as I looked across the bus, there right in front of me was a verse from the Bible. No adverts just this verse.

> Jeremiah 29.11 *"For I know the plans I have for you,"* says the Lord, *"Plans to prosper you and not to harm you, plans to give you hope and a future."*

I was stunned. The Lord had led me to see a promise that I needed just at that moment and He did it in a way that was so unusual that it had to be from Him.

I raced home and called John to tell him what had happened. He was quiet for a moment and then said, "My future is already secured and now the Lord is telling me not to worry about you, he has everything planned, so you are safe in his hands." It took the stress away from John for the little time that he had left and I carried this with me too, as I went through the process of grief and loss, sure that the Lord would show me what he wanted me to do next.

Does God really have plans for each one of us?

Going through hard experiences can drag us down and make us doubt God's love for us and, for some people, it even makes them doubt God's very existence. It is in these tough times that we need to learn to lean on the Lord for the strength to face whatever is to come. Scripture is full of wonderful insights into the way God works and it is through scripture that we can find the strength we need. Romans 8 is a wonderful chapter, full of encouragement, as it explains that when you belong to Christ you have been set free from the slavery of sin. It helps us to see what sin is and teaches us how to deal with it in every day life through our relationship with Jesus. It tells us how the Holy Spirit helps us in our weakness and, in verse 28, it says,

"And we know that God causes everything to work together for the good of those who love God and are called according to His purpose for them." (NLT)

We don't always see what God is doing in our lives as "good" but if we turn to him and seek him for comfort, guidance and understanding, we will find it.

John was finally taken into our local hospice where the whole family were able to see him. The Lord took him home early one morning and we were able to grieve together.

It took me about six months to settle into the routine of getting used to doing things alone. I was then approached by the church to house a young man named Colin who was coming to work in the church as an apprentice. I decided it would be good to share the house with someone and he settled in very well as he was in his twenties and looking forward to caring for himself and this suited us both.

About this time, a friend came up to me after the church service and announced, "God wants you in Kenya." I was astonished and asked "Why?" She replied, "I have no idea, but I have joined a team to visit an orphanage, run by a Charity, for a ten day visit and every time I think about it, your name comes into my mind. I am losing sleep, so please say you will come too." I was already supporting a young boy in the same orphanage but it had never crossed my mind that I could visit him face to face. This was out of the blue but the purpose of the trip was to work with the staff of the home on maintenance tasks and to get to know the children. This sounded very interesting and after committing it to prayer and not finding any reasons not to go, I made up my mind to join them on the trip. It was strange making the decision on my own but I attended the team meetings ready to prepare for the trip.

I discovered that another acquaintance from church was also going, giving the three of us the opportunity to get to know each other better.

I went through the first anniversary of losing John, closely followed a few days later by boarding the plane at Heathrow and my journey began.

1.2 A trip of discovery

This is what the Lord says—your Redeemer,
the Holy One of Israel:
"I am the Lord your God, who teaches you
what is best for you,
who directs you in the way you should go.
Isaiah 48:17 NIV

I had the privilege of growing up in a Christian home and I can remember clearly hearing about God and Jesus as I was growing up. I went to Sunday school but more than that, I grew up in an atmosphere where God was central to our life as a family. I saw my parents and my older brother and sister living in a way that showed that God was real and prayer and reading the Bible was all part of normal life, even if I did sometimes fall asleep during these family times! When I was 9 years old we had an evangelistic crusade in our area led by a man from the USA whose name was John Wesley White. Mr. Wesley White was talking very simply about the fact that God made us and loves us and wants us to be in his family, but we have sin in our lives and this keeps us separated from him. God is just and sin has to be punished, but if he punishes us for our sin we cannot survive. Jesus came to take that punishment for us when he died on the cross and we can now be in God's family because we have been forgiven. Believe and be saved. Even though I was young I understood the message and decided that I wanted to be in God's family too and on that day, June 10th 1956 my journey as a Christian began. Children are never too young to hear about the love God has for them.

So, joining the team on the trip to Kenya was going to be a trip of discovery.

As I indicated previously, the purpose of the visit was to do some maintenance work for the children's home. This would also give us a chance to understand the work of the Charity. We knew that their aim was to help these children in every aspect of their lives by rescuing them from life on the streets, caring for their physical needs, providing education, emotional support and showing and teaching them about the love of Jesus. In addition to maintenance work our task would be to spend time with the them, helping in any way we could. This brought home to us the real meaning of sponsoring a child as we shared in their daily life activities.

I did not know what to expect of life in a children's home. These children, who were so vulnerable, were being physically cared for and it was important for them to know that they had a heavenly father who loved and cared for them too. There would come a day when they would leave the home and would be facing life without the physical support of the home. In the book of John, he shares these words

John 1:12-13

12. But to all who believed him and accepted him, he gave the right to become children of God. 13 They are reborn—not with a physical birth resulting from human passion or plan, but a birth that comes from God. (NLT)

As children of God, we know we are not alone because we are part of His family. Providing these children with a home and family for a while was the least we could do.

The team landed at 9.00pm and the first thing that I felt was the warm air that hit us as we left the building even though it was night time and dark.

So this was Kenya. We boarded our transport and as we left the airport we were aware of some beautiful animal sculptures and then some dimly out lined real zebras in a nearby field. Our first night was in a guest house in a gated compound with a guard. It was so late we were immediately allocated our rooms. We had a good night's sleep and enjoyed breakfast together the next morning. In the daylight we were able to see the beautiful garden surrounding the guest house. After a short Bible devotion time, we were off to a supermarket for supplies.

This supermarket was similar to our own with food, clothing and daily items on sale. Although the brands were new to us the basic items were the same. We bought sweets for the children and sodas, as they were very cheap compared with prices at home and we understood that the children loved to have soda as a treat.

We began the long drive to the children's home, taking about 5-6 hours with challenging road conditions. Potholes were very large and deep so in some places the traffic had to negotiate a way round them, slowing all the traffic down. Nairobi was packed with traffic and people, it was noisy, dusty and smelled of petrol fumes. Driving seemed to be a bit haphazard with most people ignoring the usual traffic rules. As we reached the outskirts of the city the traffic eased a little but there were still crowds of people everywhere. We drove along the main road which was to take us north. It was just a two lane road and as the lorries were very slow and difficult to pass, our journey too was slow.

The countryside was beautiful. Nairobi is quite high in the landscape, approximately 6,000 feet above sea level, so we enjoyed many hills and valleys and the beautiful green fields full of unfamiliar crops. Maize seemed to be grown everywhere and we learnt that it was the staple diet for Kenyans. We saw fields of pineapples as far as the eye could see with watchtowers to deter stealing and banana trees were in abundance too.

The people would sell fruits and vegetables either by the side of the road or in open market places near small villages or towns. We stopped at one of these roadside markets to have a better look at the range of fruit and vegetables for sale and we stocked up to enjoy them later. The most dramatic incident was when we stopped in a small town where the people selling bananas would thrust large hands of them through any open window offering them for sale, they all seemed so cheap compared with prices back at home. The journey gave us time to absorb the sights, sounds and smells of Kenya, we were seeing normal everyday life, so different from our own. All the people we met would smile and want to shake our hands and they were very excited to see us.

We noticed that we were stopped several times by police checkpoints and the drivers conversed with them in Swahili. We were not aware of money changing hands but that was essentially the reason for being stopped. Was this going to be something I had to get used to during my time here I wondered? The last leg of our journey was on dirt roads with a rather precarious bridge that had seen better days but fortunately we crossed safely without incident.

We reached the home and again it was a gated compound with uniformed guards who greeted us warmly and directed us to our accommodation, the team bungalow. It nestled among trees and bushes with a small water tower close to the building. Most communities had gated compounds for security, even in the small local town there were small groups of houses with the same gated security, with or without guards.

We were tired and hungry but eager to settle into our accommodation. As we stood there waiting for our bags to be unloaded we were told that we may see a lot of safari ants and it would be wiser to wait inside the bungalow. This warning came a little late for some of us and I found myself being bitten inside my trousers at the top of my legs. I sprinted into a nearby room to remove my trousers and sure enough these large ants were not only biting but hanging on, and needed to be physically pulled off. There was no lasting discomfort, once they were gone so was the pain.

After being well fed by our hosts we met the Home manager and his senior staff, the missionary couple who were there to oversee and encourage the work and a young lady from my own church who was an intern there for six months in her gap year after high school. They took us to meet the children who had their own little village which consisted of three houses for the children and one for the doctor and his wife. These buildings formed a semi circle around a large grassy area where the children could play and between two of the houses they had an outside paved laundry area with communal large sinks and washing lines.

A glimpse of life so very different from our own.

1.3 Understanding the mission

The Lord says, "I will guide you along the
best pathway for your life.
I will advise you and watch over you.
Psalm 32:8 NLT

The children were delightful! They were very excited to see us
and even more excited to receive the sweets and sodas we gave
them. We discovered that they lived in four separate houses
arranged by age, three in this village and one for the older girls
near the main administration building. In each house there were
two dormitories, two bathrooms, a small kitchen and a larger
room for the main activities. We were invited to see their houses
and we admired the photos on the walls. These were from
sponsors and various team's visits. Each house had a house
"mother" with an extra helper for the youngest children. We
discovered all meals were served in a large dining room near the
main office and this room doubled for use as a church too.

There were actually two homes, one for girls and the
very young boys and one for older boys. They were about
30 minutes drive apart and I was told that my sponsor boy,
Adam, was living at the boys home but had been diagnosed
with mumps that very day. This did not seem to curb any of his
activities but meant that I would meet him later in the visit
when he was well again.

We had various projects to do suggested by the home
manager and his team. I was working with a group that had
been asked to provide a study area and a library for the older
children to use when doing their homework. This room was in
the main administration building. The main room was easy as
we just needed to scrub it well, give it a fresh coat of paint and

provide a long desk area. The suggested space for the library was in a small building built onto the side of the main building with inside access, more like a large cupboard. The problem was that this small structure was pulling away from the main building and we were not sure how long it would last. It had been added on without physically tying the new walls to the old building, so we ended up demolishing it completely, rebuilding it, making the proper joints to secure the structure. By the time we finished, we were able to plaster the walls and paint it all ready for the shelves and books. It was very satisfying work.

We spent the end of each day with the children once they were home from school and we enjoyed a time of games, singing, prayers and a Bible story before they went to bed. Most of the children attended local schools but we visited their 'on site' school where there were four small classes being held in a converted stable block, with two more classrooms under construction for the youngest children of the home. At the weekend, the children had chores to do, but after they were completed we were able to play running around games with them, including volleyball and basketball. On Easter Sunday we were asked to take the service for them in their own church. Local community people were encouraged to join in with these services. Several groups of children from the home entertained us with songs and I was selected to tell the Easter story with the use of a flannel graph. That took me back to my own Sunday school days!! It was very evident how much the children enjoyed this time together.

There is a strong tradition of Christianity in Kenya and it is encouraged in many areas of people's lives, particularly in schools. The two homes, run by the Charity, were both in remote areas of the bush and they each had their own church and pastor. Being able to encourage people from the local area to attend the church was very important. Good relationships were developed with other local churches throughout the area too.

The day came to visit the boys' home. We travelled deeper into the bush to a very remote place by a river. The surroundings were beautiful as both the homes were in the foothills of Mount Kenya. The approach road was quite treacherous as the ruts were so deep, but our driver manoeuvred the vehicle along the tracks with amazing skill. The boys told us tales of the wild animals in the area and they would often see elephants passing by. On one occasion a staff member was chased by an elephant but survived to tell the tale. Leopards had also been seen but without serious incidents. We later had the joy of seeing these animals when we were taken for a short safari at the end of our visit. I had started to sponsor Adam when he was seven years old and he was now thirteen. He took me on a tour of the site and I was amazed to see that the boys' dormitories had three tier bunks. I had never seen anything like these before. The accommodation was very similar to that of the girls with bathrooms and a large dining hall and a separate building for their church. We spent the day getting to know them and sharing craft activities. We made small vehicles from lolly sticks, with cardboard wheels and rubber bands and had great fun racing them around the outside of the building. It was a real joy to spend time with the boy I had only known through letters and we became firm friends. He pleaded with me to return but I could not make promises that I may not be able to keep, but my heart was definitely being affected by everything I was seeing and experiencing.

During these ten days we heard the many heart wrenching background stories of some of the children. It was very hard for some families to take on the children of siblings who had died and so many of these children often ended up on the streets. I met a little girl born illegitimately whose mother had passed away after contracting Aids. She herself was HIV positive and the wider family did not want the responsibility of bringing her up, so she came to the home. One little boy was actually found, as a baby, in a paper bag in a waste bin where he had been abandoned. Many had suffered abuse. These stories were all distressing, for many had no idea who or where their families were. Each story was unique but with the same outcome, abandoned and then rescued. The Bible verse at the heart of this organisation is

Isaiah 1:17 Learn to do right; seek justice. Defend the oppressed.

Take up the cause of the fatherless; plead the case of the widow. (NIV)

I had never been faced with such incredibly sad situations in my comfortable middle class life. I was becoming so aware of the real needs of these children and yet there was a contentment about them, because this was so much better than what they had before. But it didn't stop there. They needed healing from their emotional traumas as well as the physical provision, they needed to learn how to survive in such a world. The only real answer is in their relationship with their heavenly father.

It was not until our final day at the Home when I was looking at the view as the clouds suddenly parted that Mount Kenya was visible. This was the first time we had seen it during this ten day visit. I had been praying about the plans that God had promised for me and I had a feeling of real contentment as I took in the beautiful sight. Alongside all this I was beginning to see that maybe the future I had been promised by God could in some way be connected with Kenya.

1.4 A reason to return

God's way is perfect.
All the Lord's promises prove true.
He is a shield for all who look to him for protection.
Psalm 18:30 (NLT)

I was loving every minute of this trip, making new friends, meeting the children, meeting the staff and learning about the way of life in Kenya, The young lady from my church came to see us as we worked on the library and she asked if she could talk with me. She asked me to follow her to a locked room in the admin building. Firstly, she shared the fact that the missionary couple were preparing to go home to Canada, they had reached the age of sixty and a bout of poor health had led them to make arrangements to finish their ministry in Kenya. They were due to leave at the end of May and that would mean she would be in Kenya on her own for a whole month, as she wasn't due to go home until the end of June. Communication in those days was difficult! The cost of phoning home was prohibitive and it was only possible to use the internet at an internet cafe in the town that was thirty minutes' drive away. She had no transport and had relied on the missionaries for that support. My first instinct was to offer to come back for the month of June, so she was not alone, and to then take her home with me. We agreed that this would be the best solution if we could get the agreement of the home manager.

She then opened the locked room and showed me piles of boxes, bags and cases, full of items that had been donated by earlier teams. There were craft supplies, books, games and sports equipment. She explained that the Kenyan staff really did not know what to do with it all and it was locked away to prevent stealing. There was so much and this was like an Aladdin's cave to me, a UK primary school teacher. I told her that I knew exactly what to do with it and we needed to go and see the home manger as soon as we could.

We shared the idea of a return with my two colleagues, and they agreed to come with me, as they too would like to return. When we saw the home's manager we put forward our proposal and he was very keen for us to come back for the month of June, recognising that there would be plenty for us to do as the missionaries would be gone by then. The agreement was made and we began our goodbyes to the staff and children.

The last part of our trip was to see the animals in the safari park as I mentioned before.

We drove to the Aberdare Country Club where we were warmly greeted and had a time to relax before lunch. The daughter of the manager had worked with the Charity for a while so he was very keen to support in any way he could. There was a small swimming pool for us to enjoy and we began to see some of the local wildlife. There were warthogs, deer and noisy peacocks that wandered up to the main buildings. We had a wonderful buffet lunch and then prepared for our safari. We were in two vehicles and were taken to see the giraffes, zebras, impala and eland grazing in the grounds of the club. We were able to get out of the vehicles quite close to them as these animals were not considered dangerous, it was so delightful.

We were then taken to the main safari park, which was 767 square kilometres in size. This was such an adventure for us. The first stop was to look down into the valley at the watering hole where the Treetops lodge was situated. For us Brits it was very exciting to see the place where our late Queen first heard that her father had died and that she was then Queen of the United Kingdom. We had a drive around in search of as many animals as we could find and saw a lovely variety, elephants, wild boar, baboons, buffalo and hyenas. Here we were not allowed to leave the vehicles as they were certainly more dangerous. After a couple of hours we were about to go on to the lodge, which was incidentally in the shape of the Noah's ark, when one of our vehicles got into difficulties. As passengers we were not sure what was happening, but we knew it would soon be dark, so they called for a rescue vehicle. It was decided to put all the men into the broken down vehicle to await rescue, while all the women would be taken ahead to the Ark. We heard later, that as darkness fell, the stranded vehicle had become of great interest to the hyenas who gradually encircled it. A very dramatic way to end the day! The overnight stay at the Ark was beautiful with so many animals coming to the watering hole. It was possible to stay up all night to watch them, although most of us went to bed. They had a buzzer system to wake us, should anything unusual take place.

The drama was not over as the journey back to the airport took an unexpected turn! It began to rain and it was torrential with very heavy traffic on the roads. The ground alongside the tarmac was like a muddy, fast moving river, so it was essential to stay on the road. We were getting later and later and it was feared that we may miss our flight and so the drivers decided to take another route through the slum area where they hoped the traffic would be less. This was a dangerous place to be and by now it was dark too. We were told, as long as we kept the vehicles locked, we would be fine. The traffic came to a standstill and the driver of the other vehicle decided to take a risk by overtaking the traffic jam and driving off the road, resulting in it getting stuck in the mud. A group of men came from nowhere offering to push them out of the mud but they wanted to be paid. They got the vehicle back on the road and made their demands. They decided not enough money was being offered so they started to rock the vehicle violently.

Someone took a hand full of notes, opened the window, threw the notes into the air. All the men dived for the money. The driver put his foot down and somehow we found a way through the traffic and on to the airport in time for our flight.

This was certainly a memorable trip.

When looking for answers from the Lord, it is often easy to take verses out of context to make them say what we want to hear. So, it is always wise to read the verses in context to be sure that you have understood what is being said. Thinking over this amazing trip, these are the words that came to mind. In this part of Ephesians Paul is talking about us being made alive in Christ.

Ephesians 2:8-10

8. For it is by grace you have been saved, through faith—and this is not from yourselves, it is the gift of God— 9 not by works, so that no one can boast. 10 For we are God's handiwork, created in Christ Jesus to do good works, which God prepared in advance for us to do.

I belong to the Lord, the life I have in him is given to me by God's grace. He made me and knows me, so now my mind was beginning to see this trip, not as just a nice thing to do but, maybe, as the beginning of the next thing the Lord had prepared for my life. Is this what I have been created for in the purposes of God? With my head and heart so full, there would be much prayer needed for this.

1.5 Preparing to return

The Lord says, "I will guide you along the
best pathway for your life.
I will advise you and watch over you.
Psalm 32:8 NLT

I now had six weeks to think about the return to Kenya. I am
sure that it was the Lord who had created a reason for my
return so that I could experience more of life in Kenya.
Sometimes we forget just how much God is doing in our lives
because we take so much for granted. It seems impossible that
the creator God will be interested in the smallest detail of my
life, but he is. There are so many scriptures that tell us how
much he loves and cares for us but to apply them to ourselves
can sometimes be hard to do. Look at Psalm 23.

1. The Lord is my shepherd, I lack nothing.

2. He makes me lie down in green pastures, he leads me
beside quiet waters,

3. He refreshes my soul. He guides me along the right
paths for his name's sake.

4. Even though I walk through the darkest valley, I will
fear no evil, for you are with me your rod and your staff,
they comfort me.

I knew he was guiding me and I was looking for reassurance
that what I was seeing and understanding was really from him.

This next visit would be very different as we would not be
part of a team and we would not have any specific projects to
fill our time. I was forming a plan in my mind that I would visit

Kenya once every year and in that way I could build my
relationship with Adam, as well as taking part in any of the
work that was needed there. I talked with my family and
shared the experiences I'd had, and told them that I was
contemplating the yearly trip to Kenya.

My two colleagues and I would be travelling together and
this time, with a generous gift of air miles, we travelled from
Heathrow to Johannesburg, and from there to Nairobi.
Seventeen hours of flying. We were met at the airport and
spent the night in the guest house before our long drive to the
home where we would be staying in the recently vacated
missionary bungalow. On our arrival, we discovered that the
young lady I had come to be with was no longer there. After
the missionaries had gone home, she had become sick and the
decision was made to send her home early. We went to discuss
our plans with the home manager only to discover that three
more people were on the way to share the bungalow with
us. There would be one more young lady from the UK, and
two from the United States. We set about rearranging the
accommodation for the six of us. The two from the United
States were interns from the Moody Bible Institute and were
planning to be there for about three months. The other young
lady from the UK was there on a short term mission trip from
her church. We had a very good time together learning from
each other how the Lord had brought us this far. We shared all
the chores and after our evening time with the children we
would talk about the challenges of the day.

We spent a lot of our time with the children either in the
home or in the school. It was very interesting to see the school
at work. There were just four small classes from Standards 1-4
out of 8. We wanted to observe the use of resources in the
classroom in order to guide us as we went through the boxes
and cases in the locked store room. We then spent a lot of our
time sorting and labelling the resources. We had been given a

new room, with new shelving, on which to store the items. There was a large pit of smouldering waste away from the kitchen area, and I used it to deal with the problem of disposing of unsuitable items. I would take them to the pit and toss them in. A few hours later they would all be back in the room again, slightly charred. Apparently even if they did not know what they were, or how to use them, the Kenyan staff could not throw away anything that had been given. We understood, but these items were definitely not suitable for them, so we had to take the rubbish to the pit and watch it burn to be sure these things were gone. With the bags and boxes sorted, stored and labelled, it was now back to the school to talk with the teachers about the resources in the store room, and to make a plan too, for the best use of them. We brought them to the room and they were very excited to see what was there. However, it needed careful monitoring, so the head teacher and home manager had control of the stock.

The school was very small. Originally it was created by the home to cater for the children who were too sick to go to the local school. Several of the children were HIV positive. With no treatment, they were often too ill to attend, so schooling was intermittent. Some children were older but had come to the home without any prior education and were taught at home until they were ready for the State school. As time had passed the government had brought in free ARV (anti retro viral) medicine to treat anyone in the population who was diagnosed with HIV. This had transformed the lives of these children and it was now impossible to single out the children who were living with HIV. Having started to home school them it was decided to continue, as the nearest school was three kilometres away, and the only way to get there was to walk. So the home school was born and the youngest children were taught there. After the first four years they would transfer to the nearest State school. Our school was named after a school in the UK called Hall Mead, because a team of young people from Hall Mead had been to visit the home a few years before and had transformed the stable block into classrooms for the home schooling. The dream now was to make this school bigger for all the children to attend.

I had been a teacher for more than twenty five years but the methods of teaching were very different here, mainly rote learning. I had always worked in primary schools and I had finished my career with seven years in Early Years, 3-5 year olds. I observed that there were three children in the home who were not yet old enough to attend school and I was interested to see what they were doing during the day. I spoke to the home manager, and the carers, and explained that there were many things that could be done with these little children to encourage learning through play. I worked closely with a carer and a teacher who was also working with children with special needs and we devised some activities for all of them together. I could not verbally communicate with the children, but I could with the adults, and so I was able to demonstrate my ideas using actions and words and they in turn translated for the children. We had a great time exploring these ideas together. We also filmed them, so they could continue to explore the new methods when I had returned home.

One day a boy, about five years old, was brought into the home. He was very sick, bloated through malnutrition, and suffering kidney failure, so he could not join in with the other children. This little boy was an orphan being cared for by his grandmother, who was very old. He just stared straight ahead, not focusing on anything. I had never seen a child with no life in his eyes before. His grandmother had no idea how to give him his medication and when there was no more money, she would sell it. She did not understand just how important the medicine was and as he seemed to be fat, she assumed he did not need much food. He was so sick and near to death that the medical staff at the clinic took him straight to hospital. We did not expect to see him again. Eight days later he was back home with us. What a transformation, a lively face and a beautiful smile. He giggled at everything that was happening around him and it was such a joy to see the other children entertaining him so that they could see him laugh. As soon as he was able to walk again he joined our little group.

To see such little steps of encouragement beginning to make a difference to these children was exciting and very humbling. We take so much for granted, not really appreciating all we have ourselves. I was being drawn so much closer to the work here in Kenya.

1.6 Beyond the gates

18. The Lord is near to all who call on him,
to all who call on him in truth.
19. He fulfils the desires of those who fear him;
he hears their cry and saves them.
Psalm 145:18-19 NIV

On my first trip we had either stayed in the home, or travelled together for prearranged activities. This visit was so different. After two weeks of my month in Kenya had passed, my three UK colleagues had gone home, we three who were left were invited to have a meal with the headteacher and his wife at their home. So this would be our first outing from the home and it was an exciting prospect to see some of the everyday life of a family. My expectations were again challenged. Time, so important to us, did not matter in the same way here. We are governed by being on time, and we either wear watches, or check our phones to make sure we are keeping to time. One of the carers, Angela, was due to take two special needs children back to their boarding school. She needed transport and she also included two of their friends to travel with us. So, the car was filled with people. We were already almost at the arranged time for the meal, but I supposed that the school must be on the way, and we would just drop them off, and maybe, just be a little late. We stopped at the local market for Angela to buy some fruit, and this took some time as she liked to chat. This market was a very busy place and we soon lost sight of her. I stepped out of the vehicle to see if I could see her, but it was impossible with so many people around. I then realised I was the centre of attention, as many people began to stare in my direction. It is easy to forget that being white in a more remote area always causes a stir. Angela eventually returned and we continued to the school. We were invited in and the girls were taken to their rooms while introductions were then made to the staff, and various discussions took place. I found myself being very anxious about the time and worrying about the family we were visiting. Eventually we left the school, arriving at the head teacher's home about two hours late, and with three extra people they were not expecting. I was amazed at how they accepted the situation with no fuss at all.

Their house was behind large gates and was a small wooden structure. It had a main room and a curtained area making two bedrooms for the couple and their two children. The kitchen was a small structure just outside the main house. We all sat together in a circle in the main room where we enjoyed the meal, eating from bowls on our laps. We went for a walk to the river and back through a garden of banana trees. By now it was getting dark and time to go home. The road outside was quite narrow and reversing out was going to be difficult. It was decided that as passengers, we needed to walk ahead a little, while the car was manoeuvred onto the road. We strolled in the dark but after about half a mile we realised that something must have gone wrong. We could hear lots of revving and knew the car had gone into the ditch and it took about an hour to get it back onto the road. (This became a familiar problem over the years I spent in Kenya.) In the meantime we were sitting, in the dark, by the side of the road waiting. We encountered some local drunk men, who were very curious about us but they were turned away by Angela, who knew exactly how to deal with them. The car eventually arrived and we made our way home.

The second outing was to a larger town where they were celebrating the "Day of the African Child." I was taken with some of our children who were going to perform a recitation and a dance. I saw Adam on this day and his amazement at seeing me again was delightful. It was a very hot day and there was not much shade in the field. After we had watched the performances of many schools we had a break and Adam asked to speak to me, so we sat together on the grass. It was, as usual, quite heart wrenching to hear him tell me his story. He had a brother and sisters but he wanted me to know that he was a good boy and he asked if I could take him home with me. I had to explain to him that it was not possible to take him home, I was too old to consider caring for him, and his place was in Kenya with his brother and sisters. I did tell him that if it was possible I would come back to see him again. I had managed it once and hopefully I could do it again.

So I'd had my first glimpse of a busy town and now my first journey in a matatu, the local bus, to return to the small village within reach of the home. Back in the home I was approached by Angela and asked if I would take a Bible study with the female staff. Having been involved with a women's Bible study group at home I was very happy to do this. There were four days left in the week, so I agreed to cover those four days. We met in one of the houses and, as the local workers only had a little English and spoke Kikuyu or Swahili, I had a translator. I decided to share the book of Ruth with them, taking one chapter a day.

I love the story of Ruth with the link in the genealogy with David and Jesus.

There were some lovely lessons to learn. The love between Naomi and her daughter-in-law, Ruth, leading to Ruth's commitment to stay with Naomi and travel to a foreign land. Ruth had no idea what to expect but was content to serve her mother-in-law without the promise of reward. She committed herself to her mother-in-law and to the God whom she served. Her relationship was growing with Boaz, who knew and understood what Ruth was facing, as his own mother was also a foreigner who had been accepted into God's family.

They received the blessing of a child who would one day lead to the coming of Jesus.

During the studies I decided I would do what I did back at home, and that was to teach and then ask questions. All I got was a blank stare. I realised that I was not going to get any kind of conversation, so I had to tailor my talks to be just teaching. It was hard work with no responses, and I could not even read their body language or faces. By the end of the week, I felt as if I had failed to engage these ladies at all, although my translator told me how much she had enjoyed it. I presumed she was being polite. I was so thankful that it was over. A couple of days later I met one of the ladies in the lane leading to the gates and she asked me, "Are you coming back to teach us more? We really enjoyed learning from you." I was very bemused to hear that they had actually enjoyed it. I decided I needed to find out why I got no response and was told that in the classroom, in Kenya, you are not allowed to speak. The teacher teaches and you listen, so it would have been very rude to speak out. I had many things to learn about life in Kenya!!

Now I was faced with these things to consider as the Lord was gradually revealing his plans to me.

- The Lord had shown me that maybe my skills as a teacher could be used. We all have God given talents that He can use.

- He had also shown me that the women could learn from me.

- He had stirred a love for Adam in my heart that made me want to come back to see him again.

I was reminded of the verse in *Psalm 37:4 Take delight in the Lord, and he will give you the desires of your heart.*

I had always thought about the desires of my heart being something that I wanted, and he would give me, but I suddenly thought that actually God was directing the desires of my heart. He was planting the desires in my heart and I was getting a little overwhelmed. He was opening my eyes to see a world so far from the one where I had lived all my life. He was showing me people who had so little compared to what I had. He was showing me a life not governed by the structures and pressures I was used to. What on earth could my place be in all of this? The most amazing thing to me was that I really wanted to be in Kenya.

2. Learning to live in a different culture

2.1 What next?

*Wait for the Lord; be strong and take heart
and wait for the Lord.*
Psalm 27:14 NIV

It was strange being back home with so many things on my mind. I now needed to prayerfully work my way through all the experiences and feelings I had. I needed to be certain that this was the Lord's plan for me.

I recalled, years before, we'd had a conference held in my church one Saturday. People from many churches around had come and we had some sessions where we discussed various questions with the person nearest to us, preferably someone we did not know. I found myself in discussion with a lady who had retired and gone to serve the Lord in South America. She was a widow and had a family. I asked her how she could bear to leave her family and go so very far away. She told me that she needed to be obedient to the Lord and this was what he had chosen for her to do. I remember thinking, "There is no way that I could do that, to leave my children and grandchildren would not be an option for me." It was one of those ideas I dismissed as being a step too far.

Now I was facing the same prospect. So, obedience was the key. On the face of it, the Lord knew that I could do the job and was offering me the chance to follow a plan that he had mapped out for me. He was still giving me the chance to be obedient to this plan or not. God's purposes would be fulfilled with or without me. He was offering me the privilege of serving him in this particular place, at this particular time. The question was, would I be willing to be obedient?

There are so many wonderful examples in the Bible of people willing to be obedient to the Lord.

In Genesis 12:1 this is what God said to Abraham, "Go from your country, your people and your father's household to the land I will show you.

He also made some wonderful promises.

2. "I will make you into a great nation, and I will bless you; I will make your name great, and you will be a blessing. 3. I will bless those who bless you, and whoever curses you I will curse; and all peoples on earth will be blessed through you."

Abraham was not only obedient but he had a faith that believed every word God said.

So, prayerfully thinking all this through, I was willing to obey God but unsure of the timescale, I was already 60 years old so time would be limited. So why did I think the Lord wanted me there? I could see myself helping in the school and maybe some Bible teaching with the women. It was hard to pin anything down, but the yearning in my heart to go back was strong. I had begun to love these children and wanted to help them.

Guidance can be quite a hot topic in Christian circles but I had a wonderful mother who taught me to take everything to the Lord in prayer. Having talked it through with the Lord, move forward in the direction you would most like to go, and trust that if it was not right the Lord would close the door.

In Isaiah 48:17 the Lord is talking to his people. He has struggled with them for so long and wants them to understand how much he cares for them.

This is what the Lord says—your Redeemer, the Holy One of Israel:

"I am the Lord your God, who teaches you what is best for you, who directs you in the way you should go.

I wanted so much to do the right thing. I wanted God to teach and direct me. God had been so faithful to my family and had held us close through the loss of John.

I approached the Charity that had originally sent the team and I was encouraged to pursue the idea. I then wrote to the director of the work in Kenya to put before her the possibility of going back. The reply stunned me beyond belief. She was very polite and thanked me for my offer, but explained that another Christian family would be coming very soon and the things I had mentioned as possible areas of work would be covered by the family, and there would be no place for me.

My head was spinning. It never occurred to me that I would be turned down. I was so disappointed, but I had to sit down and work my way through this disappointment. I had been so sure the Lord was leading me in this direction and I felt he stirred in me a desire that had not been there before. This is where faith is tested. I really did believe that God had a plan for me and I had assumed this was it. Now I had to continue with prayer, and see where the Lord would take me next.

It now looked as if it would be a once a year, team visit. I prayed and asked God what was happening? There were no quick easy answers and no blinding lights of revelation. I now had to accept the fact that it was not for me. I had to look to the future and continue to seek out his plans for me.

I decided that I just needed to pray for Kenya, and all the people I had met, and trust the Lord that if he ever wanted me to go, I was ready and willing. So for the next few months I settled back into the work I had been doing with our women's group and making Sunday school leaflets. I was also asked to consider working with the youngest group of children on a Sunday. I was hesitant to do this but it was under consideration. I needed to concentrate on my relationship with the Lord himself.

2.2 Opening doors

4. Take delight in the Lord,
and he will give you the desires of your heart.
5. Commit your way to the Lord;
trust in him and he will do this:
Psalm 37:4-5 NIV

One day in October I had a phone call telling me that the home manager, Mark, and two children from the home I had stayed in, would be coming to the UK. They would be on a two week visit and would I like to help? They were to visit a school in Canning Town, London where the children would experience being in an English school and Mark would observe the day to day life of the school. They had already been in attendance at the school for three days but they wanted to be sure Mark was understanding what he was seeing, as teaching methods in Kenya were different. Mark was a qualified teacher himself so he was finding the visit very useful.

I drove them to the school and we had a good conversation with the Head Teacher of the school with whom we planned the activities for the day. The children went to their class and worked alongside the other children. It was quite a challenge, as at home in Kenya, learning in English didn't start until year 4 although these children had been exposed to more English through the home.

I escorted Mark to each allocated lesson and we looked at the objectives and classroom activities. We also went outside to observe the playground games. We had lunch together with the staff and then Mark asked me to go back to the Early Years department where he asked questions about what he could see from the layout of the area and the activities that had been planned. As I had previously discovered, learning through play was not usually practiced. When we had finished talking, Mark turned to me and said, "Please come back to Kenya and teach my teachers how to do this." My answer was an immediate "Yes". I felt as if this was what I had been waiting for. It was the real purpose for my return. We talked over the details during the following week as we went sightseeing in and around London.

It was decided that I would return on January 1st, so I had a couple of months to prepare. By now I had two young men living in my house and one of them was getting married in June so I planned to be in Kenya for 5 months so that I could be back for the wedding. I was sure I could achieve a lot in that time! This was such an exciting prospect for me, and of course I had to turn down the idea of working with the youngest children in church. My other jobs too had to be handed over. I think most people were bemused, and unknown to me, some people were very worried that I was rushing into something that I had not considered properly, but of course they had not been aware of how much prayer had gone into this decision.

There were so many things to think about but I steadily worked through the list. The house would be ok, as the two young men from church living in the house would take care of it for me. They would continue, looking after themselves and the house. Now I needed to decide what to do with my car. I was on may way to church just before Christmas and met a young woman from my Bible study group. I was explaining that I needed someone to drive my car while I was away so that it didn't die and she was very happy to do that for me. I would leave my car outside the house and she would collect it after I had gone.

Then disaster happened. I was planning to meet with a very close friend for lunch and I was busy in the kitchen. I was happily grating some cheese and managed to take a chunk of flesh from my thumb. I was bleeding profusely by the time she arrived. She hurried me to my doctor where it was decided that it was more than they could cope with and sent me straight to A&E at the local hospital. We arrived at 2.00pm and I persuaded my friend to leave me there as it could be a very long wait. It was, and my thumb still had not stopped bleeding. After I had been examined they decided that it was not possible for them to treat me and I would need to go to another hospital for plastic surgery the following day. By now it was 9.00pm and I was about to call for a taxi when another good friend called and offered to take me home, and then on to the second hospital appointment the following day. I had to sleep in an upright position.

The following day was just as difficult. They decided that they could not repair the damage because it was too close to the thumb nail. They filled the hole with a cream and dressed it with bandages. I explained that I was about to leave for Kenya so they gave me detailed instructions and a large supply of cream and bandages. I intended to use the clinic on site in Kenya to have it checked regularly. My next appointment at this hospital would be in June when I returned and they hoped to sign me off.

Everything seemed to be happening so fast. Tickets were bought, goodbyes said and friends took me to the airport. I had been so preoccupied with my preparations that I had not taken any notice of the news and I had no idea of the chaos that I would be flying into. I had a vague recollection that there was an election but I never dreamed that it would be violent. I would be flying into a country where I would not have the normal protections I was so used to, and I had no idea of the many lessons the Lord had planned for me to learn apart from the work I would be doing to help others. I was committed now for the next five months so I would just concentrate on that.

2.3 A very different Kenya

Respect everyone, and love the family of believers.
Fear God, and respect the king.
1 Peter 2:17 NLT

I had been learning how to listen to the Lord through his word and seeing just how true his word is in our lives. I had to understand that he had definite things for me to do, but I needed to be sure that I understood what was being said to me. Having been convinced, I then needed to wait until God showed the way forward clearly.

God does not promise us an easy life. Jesus actually says in

Luke 9:23 Then he said to them all: 'Whoever wants to be my disciple must deny themselves and take up their cross daily and follow me'.

In fact we should expect all the same difficulties and troubles the world throws at us but if you are a follower of Jesus, we don't face any of them alone. Those who tell you, "Come to Jesus and all your troubles will go away", are not telling the truth.

1 Corinthians 10:13 No temptation has overtaken you except what is common to mankind. And God is faithful; he will not let you be tempted beyond what you can bear. But when you are tempted, he will also provide a way out so that you can endure it.

So we still have to face the same difficulties as anyone else. I needed to understand that the Lord would really be with me, close to me and caring for me. I was unaware at that time, I would be the only white person for miles around. I had so much to learn moving into a culture that I didn't really understand.

So here I was again, the plane coming in to land at Nairobi airport, not knowing if my friends would be there. In all the preparations to come to Kenya it never once dawned on me that this could be a dangerous thing to do. The word elections did not conjure up riots in my mind so this was definitely a shock. Elections had not been this violent before in Kenya, so everyone was in shock. I waited in line to go through passport control and I was relieved to find that all was normal and my Kenyan friends were waiting for me. Nairobi was eerily empty and we only saw about five other cars. We were stopped at various checkpoints by armed police and soldiers who asked who we were and where we were going. My friends had taken a very circuitous route to the airport to avoid any trouble spots and we retraced it to reach the guest house for our overnight stay.

When we reached the guest house we found all was calm and quiet. Nairobi is normally a very busy congested city, so to be driving through the following day without seeing any other cars was very strange. All the shops were shut and not one person was seen walking about. As we left the city we were stopped again by police and soldiers at various checkpoints. They were very polite and we were able to make good progress.

There were two main parties in the election with the Kikuyu leader, Kibaki, apparently winning against Raila who was leading the opposition. They were both accused of manipulation which was verified by international observers, and after consideration, Kibaki was sworn in. This was when the troubles erupted and many people were killed during the ensuing riots. On the day we were driving to the home we heard that a church full of 50 women and children, who had gone there looking for sanctuary, was burned to the ground in a tribal attack.

The trouble was fierce but the deeper we went into the Kikuyu Province, the more normal life seemed to be. We now saw shops and market stalls open with plenty of people milling around. The countryside was just as beautiful as ever and it was hard to imagine that there was such strife in the city. The journey took the usual 5 hours and the first thing I had to do on arrival was to ring my family to reassure them that I was safe.

Over the coming weeks we heard of many tragic things happening. The whole country seemed to be fighting, one tribe against another for no other reason than their tribal heritage. People who had been good neighbours now hated each other, and people were often chased away from their homes, having to make the long journey back to their own tribal homelands, leaving many of their possessions behind. We had some staff members working in the homes who had been living peacefully in the local town, but now, they were themselves under threat for their lives. Some of them came to live in our compound, as it was the only safe place for them to be. Over the following months these friends had to return to their tribal homelands, which was hard because they were leaving paid employment, not knowing whether they would find another job. We heard of Kikuyu refugees returning to their roots but with nowhere to live. Seven new settlements had been created, far away from us, to accommodate them all. The living conditions were harsh because the land they were offered was so dry and barren. There were no trees for natural shelter from the sun and all amenities were so far away. Over the following years, these communities gradually developed into working communities through hard work and commitment to each other and a desire to survive.

James 3:13 speaks of wisdom and humility.

"Who is wise and understanding among you? Let them show it by their good life, by deeds done in the humility that comes from wisdom."

Over the years I have observed how easy it is to make assumptions about people whose lives are so different from my own. This can be regarded as rather arrogant and unfeeling, and is often born of a distinct lack of respect for them.

I needed to find a way to look, listen and learn rather than speak too soon. I certainly needed the wisdom that God would provide.

2.4 Reuptation

1. A good name is more desirable than great riches;
to be esteemed is better than silver or gold.
2. Rich and poor have this in common:
The Lord is the Maker of them all.
Proverbs 22:1-2 NIV

I had the opportunity to go to Nairobi and while there, I went
to visit the Museum. This was a fascinating place and I was
able to learn a lot about the Kenyan history. Recorded history
was limited, so historic buildings were not very old, compared
with our own, and much of the culture was handed down by
word of mouth. A lot of the really early information was as a
result of exploration which seems to have started in the 19th
century. The British became involved in Kenya in 1880s making
them a Protectorate in 1895. In my own opinion, from the
things I saw and read at the museum, we did not do a very
good job. We obviously looked down on these people, many
taking advantage of them to give themselves a comfortable
existence and further commercial interests. We missed
opportunities to educate them and to help them develop for
themselves. It was not surprising that eventually there was a
Mau Mau rebellion against the authority of the British in
1952. The home where I was living was above an area now
occupied by a high school and they very kindly allowed us to
explore some of the area by the river. This area had carved
rocks and small caves where, we were told, the Mau Mau had
used the caves to hide their leaders. We also visited another
area near the boys home where again a large number of Mau
Mau warriors would hide out, being fed by the local people. In
the large Aberdare Safari Park we also saw evidence of places

where they would leave messages for one another during the fighting.

The reputation of the British was very poor as the people felt oppressed. Large areas of land had been commandeered to make huge coffee and tea plantations and the people were employed to work there for poor wages. This meant that the land, so highly prized as family land, was lost to the generations who would follow. Owning a piece of land for your family to inherit is still considered to be the way for your family to flourish, and building a house, however modest, is the goal for many people.

When I was first in Kenya I was asked to register my presence so that if there should be any further troubles, I could be rescued. I was given a place to go to where we would be airlifted out. This turned out to be the Aberdare Country Club which had its own helicopter pad, plus there was a small airfield nearby. I had to go there to register. I met a British man, who had lived in Kenya for many years, and we had a very enjoyable conversation over coffee. As the name implies, this was an exclusive club during the British rule. There was a golf course, tennis courts and a swimming pool, plus there was a main building housing offices and a restaurant, with small lodges built in the grounds for people to stay. It was absolutely beautiful, with amazing views and animals wandering around in the grounds. Thankfully it was no longer exclusive.

There were occasions when I would meet someone who was obviously very anti British but amazingly most of the time I was greeted very warmly and treated with respect.

Reputations are very precious and constantly we read in the Bible about God's reputation. 'The name of the Lord' is important and 'You shall not misuse the name of the Lord' is one of the commandments. We are commended to call on the name of the Lord or praise the name of the Lord. He told his people that he needed to protect the honour of his name.

The power of God was known everywhere and in Jericho when the spies went to the house of Rahab, she said to them,

> *"I know that the Lord has given you this land and that a great fear of you has fallen on us, so that all who live in this country are melting in fear because of you. 10. We have heard how the Lord dried up the water of the Red Sea for you when you came out of Egypt"*

That was 40 years before but the people of Jericho had not forgotten and God's reputation as the God of the Israelites was one to be feared.

I also discovered that there were times when people refused to serve me because of the reputation of white people who had been there before me, so I had to begin again to build trust with them and repair the damage to the name of the Charity. I realised very early on that my behaviour was really crucial for the reputation of the Charity I was serving, and also that my behaviour should reflect the words that came out of my mouth.

So, I was learning that it was really important not to have an attitude of superiority. One of the biggest mistakes was to imagine that what I had to offer was better than what they already had. I had to understand the culture, so I began with observation. So, within the realm of the classroom I would ask questions and commended good practice wherever possible. I needed to know why things were done in a certain way, and saw that there were often really good reasons. We would then talk after a lesson, on equal terms, learning from each other. I was then able to offer ideas that would help, rather than try to impose them from my own perspective. By doing this, I was able to grow some really firm friendships.

I was invited to several homes for a cup of tea or a meal. These homes varied from a mud hut with dirt floor; a wooden hut with a dirt floor; to a block-built house with wooden or concrete floors. In all circumstances the hospitality was delightful. There was a real sense of pride in their own surroundings, wanting to share what they had and I learned to really appreciate these visits. I grew to enjoy the milky sweet tea and the Kenyan food. It was a really special day when team visitors were coming, but they always reminded me, "Mum don't forget you are one of us now". I discovered that I did have a reputation among the community, all of whom knew me even if I did not know them. I would often stop to give people a lift in my car, if they were walking in my direction, as the roads were long and rough. They would say "Thank you Madam Ruth" I can remember saying "Do I know you?" and they would say "No, but we know you."

Christians can often have a bad name, being intolerant, judgemental, bigoted. We are told in Romans 12:18 '*If it is possible, as far as it depends on you, live at peace with everyone.*' We need to display the fruit of the Spirit in our lives to reflect the fact that God lives in us.

2.5 Looking and learning

Finally, all of you should be of one mind.
Sympathise with each other.
Love each other as brothers and sisters.
Be tenderhearted, and keep a humble attitude.
1 Peter 3:8 NLT

My new life in Kenya began back in the bungalow I had shared with my friends, but this time I was alone. Having started to get used to being alone back in the UK I did not anticipate any particular difficulties back in Kenya. However I had not taken into consideration everything we consider as normal not really being available to me now.

I had to get used to the noises of the night, so very different from home with unidentified howling, scratching, rumblings and thumping across the roof, all outside in the pitch dark. I had my laptop with me and relied on that, to begin with, for company. I had basic amenities such as a cooker run on bottled gas, a fridge with a freezer compartment, pots and pans etc. I had been to the shop in a town called Karatina, on the way from Nairobi, to get basic food supplies. I had a small bathroom with a shower and toilet, but I had to get used to clearing blockages myself when they occurred. There was also a small tank for a water supply.

I had not been prepared for the number of strange insects and creatures who shared the bungalow with me. There was a particular caterpillar that curled up like a catherine wheel when touched; very large, very flat spiders; moths the size of a saucer, ants, cockroaches and small lizards. It became very clear that I needed to inspect my bed before getting in each night to make sure I was alone and, if I needed water in the night, I kept a bottle rather than an open glass beside the bed. I decided quite quickly that a mosquito net would be a good idea, not for mosquitoes as we didn't see many of those but just to keep my bed clear generally. One night after rain we had an invasion of flying termites, who seemed to want to attack the bungalow and started to force their way under the door. They had been attracted by the light from the windows and I spent a couple of hours fighting back by stuffing old newspaper under the door to block any gaps I could find, but they continually found tiny ways to get in. I had insect spray to kill them as they shed their wings and proceeded into the bungalow. The next morning the veranda was littered with thousands of discarded wings and it wasn't until years later, it was discovered that the disappearing termites were going under the bungalow and munching on the wooden framework of the building. Many of the insect attacks were seasonal, thankfully, so we saw fly, ant and termite seasons.

I liked the lizards, especially knowing that they would be feeding on some of these insects.

I was taken to the nearest small town to buy food and became familiar with the market and tiny grocer's shop. Sometimes, we went to a bigger town where we had a butcher, and a slightly bigger supermarket. It was funny going back to asking the butcher for a particular cut of meat, just like we used to when I was a child. He would have several carcasses hanging in the window and he would carve off the meat that was requested. I found the hardware shops very useful for screws, nails and light bulbs etc., as needs arose. I was taken to various places to meet traders who were very helpful during the subsequent years.

I registered at the bank and opened an account. I had to get used to very long queues if I needed to go there. I bought a mobile phone and registered that too, as it was the main way to keep in touch with anyone on the 50 acre site. It was also a way to keep money on hand should it be needed quickly. There was a system called Mpesa, meaning mobile money, which made it possible to send and receive money by phone. The staff in the home really looked after me and were able to introduce me to many people who would become my friends and help me should I need it. I was learning very quickly to respect the way things were done. I had to accept the limitations and use my days accordingly. I had a visit one evening from Mark the home manager who said how concerned he was that I had not laid down boundaries. I was rather confused, so I asked him, "What kind of boundaries am I supposed to put down?" He told me that missionaries would always give them boundaries, so they are not disturbed before and after certain times, and limits on who can and can't visit them in their home. At this point I did not see myself as a missionary, as this word had not been used to describe me at any time. I reassured him that anyone could come at any time to see me. I reminded him that I was alone, and as far as I was concerned, they were my friends and would always be welcome. I would turn them away if it was not convenient for me to see them, but I cannot recall ever needing to do that. In fact, it was helpful to have people coming to see me in the evenings and I was able to learn so much about the way things worked in this country. It was always important to show respect and to discuss needs through the manager and the community chief because what we see as a need, may not be a need to them. Our priorities are very different.

I also found that people would come to me for advice. This was a bit daunting at first, as I was still learning how people dealt with life in general. I realised that being old and white somehow put me in this position and it was nothing to do with any wisdom I may or may not have. The wisdom was assumed. I knew that I had to give godly answers, so this drove me to my Bible, and if I did not have an answer to give, I would tell them to come back the next day after I had had time to look at God's way of dealing with the problem. This was so good for me and I found myself always seeking the Lord's answer every day as I worked my way through the complexities of life.

I also had to learn not to run away from problems where I could not see the answer. One young man sent me a message to meet me as he needed advice. I knew the problem because it had been discussed by the management and he was about to lose his job. The decision was the right one but I did not want to get involved. I ignored the message, and decided to go to the school, as he would not come there to find me and that way I could avoid him. I carefully got everything ready for the day so I would not have to go home, and off I went early. Arriving at the school I unpacked my things and noticed that I had left one vital thing back in my house. I knew immediately that the Lord was sending me back and the young man would be waiting for me. Sure enough as I went down the short lane to the gates of the home, there he was waiting. I prayed that the Lord would help me to be obedient now, and show me what to say. He poured out his heart to me explaining that he understood why he needed to go but felt so helpless he could not think straight. He was in the final semester of a degree and was due to give a presentation that day in college. He told me he couldn't go to college because he could not think clearly enough to deliver his presentation. We talked about his Christian commitment and exactly what it meant to have a relationship with the Lord. I told him that all I could do was to tell how faithful the Lord had been to me through the most difficult times of my life. He listened and we prayed together. He then said, "Thank you so much, now I am ready to go to College." He went, gave his presentation and was given a special award as it was so good. I was so humbled by this. I should have been obedient and the Lord graciously pushed me so that I would understand why being obedient to him is so important, not just for me but to anyone else I may be interacting with.

2.6 School

Each time he said, "My grace is all you need.
My power works best in weakness."
So now I am glad to boast about my weaknesses,
so that the power of Christ can work through me.
2 Corinthians 12:9 NLT

Now it was time for the work to begin. I was very confident because this had been my area of work for the past 25 years.

My daily routine began with devotions with the staff once the children were off to school.

I would then go to the school to observe the teaching, which was informative, but so very different to the way we taught at home. This was rote learning and, from my observations, I could see that once the content was taught an assumption was made that they had all taken in the information. It was very much dependent on the blackboard and copying the information into a book.

I watched a daily routine of teaching the numbers one to ten using fingers. They also used 10 children standing at the front of the room. When I later questioned the children individually about the numbers, I discovered that they were assuming that the finger or the child who was pointed to as number one was called one and the finger or child that was pointed to as number ten was called ten. They had no idea about quantity.

I began to work alongside the teachers, with very simple activities, to help keep the children engaged in their learning and to try and establish just how much was being understood by the children. There was a formula for some teachers, where they ploughed on regardless because they were imparting the information as given in the teacher's book. I could see the gaps in the learning but how could I get this across to the teachers? I had been so confident that this was going to be straightforward but now I was beginning to understand that the teachers' own experience was so limited that the normal things I would do just did not make sense to them.

I brought a large floor puzzle to the classroom to teach the children in small groups to look at the shapes of the pieces, look at the colour and together we would make the picture. I did this every day with different groups of children. The teacher had never seen a jigsaw puzzle before and could not see or understand the value of this task. In the UK we had always understood that to make puzzles would help with concentration, short term memory, problem solving and spatial awareness. This was always seen as a way to help with children's reading skills. My intention had been to give the children table jigsaws as an activity while the teacher worked closely with a smaller group of children. I entered the room one day to find that the teacher had given every child a piece of puzzle and they were all looking to the teacher for the next move. She had no idea what to do with them.

So my challenge was how to introduce the idea of activities in the classroom not just blackboard learning. After a couple weeks, I decided to invite the teachers to my house on Saturday morning to watch a video of Early Years learning in the UK. The very task that I had been asked to accomplish in Kenya, "Teach my teachers how to do this".

They arrived and we had tea together and then watched the video. I was hoping that we could do some planning together for the coming weeks as my time with them was limited. They loved the video, but really marvelled at the equipment we worked with, and they really missed the point of learning through play, as they couldn't reproduce what they had seen. I urged them to look at what they did have and work from there.

It had been a tough morning and when they had left I almost cried as I prayed. The Lord had given me an impossible task, I might just as well go home now. How was I ever going to get through to these teachers who had no background of their own to draw on. About ten minutes later there was a knock at the door and one of the teachers had returned to say, "Please be patient with us, we really do want to learn." She became one of our greatest successes in the development of the school.

I felt that I needed to gain more insight into education in Kenya and so I visited local schools, particularly where our older children were attending. The classrooms were block built but still had the dirt floors and the windows were high so that the children would not be distracted by things happening outside. There was nothing on the walls. The children were squeezed, three into a desk made for two, so the numbers of children in each class were large, anything from 50-80 children. In the staffroom the books waiting to be marked were piled high. Now I could see why rote learning was the normal way of teaching with so many children to control in the classroom. That way each child would complete the classroom lesson and marking the books would reveal their understanding. I had a good time with the teachers and I realised that they had no time to go back over lessons if the children had not understood, as the curriculum was so full. The children would be given homework when it was hoped they would have time to assimilate the lesson, so now I could fully appreciate the desire to have our own school.

The next thing for me was to find the actual official teachers manuals in order to spend time looking at what was expected of a teacher in Kenya. This involved a trip to Nairobi with the Pastor who was appointed to drive me and guide me when I was there. We booked into a Christian guest house to stay overnight. We left early in the morning and made our way to the shopping mall where there was a large bookshop, and with the help of the staff I found the books that I needed. I also managed to find Early Years manuals. The education system took children in at Standard 1, aged 5/6 paid for by the government, but anything under Standard 1 was paid for by the parents of the children. Most interesting to me was that the curriculum for the youngest children was really good and did involve learning through play, the problem seemed to be that the teachers did not know how to put this into practice and often their employers just wanted the rote learning.

On the way back from Nairobi we reached the nearest village to the home at about 10.00pm and, as we turned into the dirt road, we had about another three kilometres to go. We had not gone very far when the pastor stopped the car and said, "I live here, so you can drive the rest of the way from here." and he was gone. This car was automatic and I had never driven an automatic car before but I had been observing how he was driving and hoped I could get this right. It was pitch black and I had to remember the route too, so I moved forward praying all the time that the Lord would be my guide!!! Such a rough road with so many large potholes. I had to remember the turning to the left and then there was the precarious bridge. I made it to the home with great relief and from the next day I was told I could borrow the car whenever I needed to. This invitation to drive was also extended to the use of the ambulance, a larger vehicle that could carry up to 14 people and had been provided to drive our HIV children to their regular hospital appointments.

This proved to be very useful because now I could visit the boys home to observe the home schooling taking place there. This was such a useful time too, as I discovered the early teaching taking place was very good. The teacher was so keen to learn from me and she put ideas into practice, even extending their use to other areas of the curriculum, with her small group of children. This was so encouraging for me. Being here in

Kenya for five months had taught me much and the every day life of my new friends and colleagues had been a real revelation to me. Reminding me so much of my own childhood days, mixed in with some of the new technology.

Through God's grace I recognised that,

- I was beginning to understand the culture.

- My respect for my colleagues had grown enormously.

- My desire to be here was firmly planted in my heart.

As the time to go home was drawing closer I wondered what would happen to the simple changes that I had been able to make. We decided that it would be helpful to bring one of the young teachers to the UK to see teaching there for himself.

I knew I would be coming back and what better idea than to have my own car. I prayed that the Lord would help me through the minefield of buying a car before I went home. I had a Christian car dealer recommended to me and made an appointment to see him. He asked me to describe the car I would like. 4x4, manual transmission, roof rack.... He had one in the carpark outside. One missionary owner and in good condition. We went for a drive in it together. He told me he would thoroughly service the car and it would be ready for me to collect when I came back.

3. Learning the cost of commitment

3.1 The future

For I can do everything through Christ,
who gives me strength.
Philippians 4:13 NLT

Now I wanted so much to be following the Lord's plans for me, I found myself spending more time in Bible reading and prayer which was building me up for the future.

I was learning that what really mattered was obedience to the Lord and not knowing what was ahead of me was not a barrier. I was following a Lord who had everything planned and all I needed to do was go forward in faith.

Reading the Bible and praying is our conversation with our Heavenly Father. We begin to see and hear the things he wants us to know. There is no substitute for spending time with him this way.

In Psalm 32:8-11 (NLT) there is this wonderful promise.

> *'The Lord says, "I will guide you along the best pathway for your life. I will advise you and watch over you.'*
>
> *9 Do not be like a senseless horse or mule that needs a bit and bridle to keep it under control."*
>
> *10 Many sorrows come to the wicked, but unfailing love surrounds those who trust the Lord.*
>
> *11 So rejoice in the Lord and be glad, all you who obey him! Shout for joy, all you whose hearts are pure!*

So we made it home to the UK. Everything there was so new to Nathan it was a joy to be able to show him around. I had a very strange experience on my first day back at home when I drove to my local supermarket to get some shopping. As I reached the door I found I could not go in! It was so huge and there was so much food on offer that I felt totally unable to make choices, so I went home again. I had heard of this phenomenon but I did not expect to experience it myself. It was like a reverse cultural shock. After a good night's sleep however, I went again the next day and was able to make my purchases.

We had a wonderful welcome from my church fellowship and Nathan made many new friends. It was evident that it was as amazing to him as my time in Kenya had been for me. We were to stay for three weeks and the purpose of the visit was to show him how schools operate in the UK. So, as one of my previous companions to Kenya was back at work, teaching at my old school, we decided to take him there for him to make some observations. The Head Teacher was very co-operative and we received a warm welcome from everyone. We visited each year group, in order to enable him to see how things were organised. It was quite a cultural shock for him to be observing in a school for 750 pupils, rather than the 30, or so, he was used to back in Kenya. We visited each classroom and were able to enjoy observing a lesson. Nathan was eager to learn, and began to understand some of the things I had been talking about as we shared these experiences together. We went sightseeing in London and even had an exclusive view of Prince Charles, as he was then, who was just coming onto the Mall in his limousine. We waved and he waved back, "He will be King one day", I told Nathan. He was able to visit some of the people he had previously met in Kenya, much to the delight of everyone. It was a very worthwhile visit for him, and he was eager to share the things he had learned, with the other teachers, when he got back home.

I now had some serious thinking to do. Back home in England my house was being shared by 2 young men, Colin and Harry who were apprentices at my church. I had timed my return specifically so that I could attend the wedding of Colin and Jane, a beautiful occasion this turned out to be. Harry, having completed his apprenticeship, was preparing to go Lebanon with the same Charity that I was working with, so now I had to decide what to do.

This was such a serious decision to make because of the consequences to my own family. Also, if I went back to Kenya, Ann my colleague from school, wanted to come with me which added to my dilemma. After much prayer I decided that I would have to return for a much longer period and so I had to break the news to my family. It was not an easy decision as I would be so far away from my family and my growing grandchildren. I still felt driven, even though the task was so tough, and I knew that if there were any changes to be made in Kenya, then I would need to commit myself to a longer term of service. I decided to sign up for a period of 3 years. I explained to my own children that I would always be ready to come home, should they need me, and that they must not hesitate to ask. Originally, I had told them that I would be visiting Kenya every year and as my eldest daughter commented, it now looked like I would be visiting the UK every year. This was one of the hardest sacrifices I have ever made. All my children lived away from me but I could always go and see them, now my visits would be limited to once a year. However, they all three, were very encouraging and supportive for me to go, which made my decision much easier.

3.2 Commitment

He gave his life to free us from every kind of sin,
to cleanse us, and to make us his very own people,
totally committed to doing good deeds.
Titus 2:14 NLT

Ann, who was from Australia and had also been with me in Kenya, was preparing to return home and had decided that she would like to spend 6 months with me in Kenya on the way. It was good to be returning with another teacher as we could share so much of the burden together.

To make things easier, she moved into my house with me, and we were then able to make our plans together. It was exciting to see how the Lord was directing each of us. Harry was now going to be working in a school in Lebanon. All three of us worked together in the same school in the UK, although in different year groups and we were now planning to work for the same Charity, although in two different countries. I felt that I now had a better understanding of the life before me, without many of the things I had always taken for granted. As I have noted before, communication was going to be difficult as the use of the mobile phone was expensive when making international calls, but it is essential to have a phone for local communication in Kenya as it was quite easy to become stranded. The internet was almost non existent at the home but we could use the internet cafe in the town. We talked to our church family about our plans and many people were keen to pray for us and signed up for a prayer letter, some were even talking about visiting too.

At the back of my mind was the fact that I was going to be away for some time and there would be no one living in the house. I committed this to the Lord and then just left it with him, but kept my eyes and ears open. The arrangement about the car was to continue and they would return it to me every time I came home. It was a perfect solution for me.

One day I was invited to a barbecue birthday party, whilst there I was told there was a young man named Paul cooking at the grill, who had come over from the States for a few weeks, and he would be returning the next day. It was suggested that I should meet him. He was a very pleasant young man who originated from India. He worked for an engineering company and had been in the States for 5 years and was soon transferring to the UK. He had been over here for a few weeks looking for accommodation and had been to see a few house shares. Sadly, in each of those, there were no Christian young people in the house and he was always offered the smallest room. He was obviously very disheartened by the whole experience, so I asked him if he would like to live in my house as I needed someone to look after it. He was rather taken aback, so I suggested that we should walk around the corner to look at my house together. To be offered a four bedroomed house instead of a small room was astonishing to him. He was so amazed that God had answered his prayer, and mine, in such a spectacular way that when he went back to his church in the States he gave testimony to them, of God's amazing answer to his prayer. Belonging to the family of God has wonderful blessings.

He returned in August and stayed with some friends while waiting for us to vacate the house but he spent every day with us getting used to his new surroundings. Another church apprentice, Michael, asked if he could live in my house too, and as there were four bedrooms I agreed. I had another old car sitting in the drive so I gave that to him for his use while I was away. I was collecting together the things I wanted with me, bearing in mind that this time I would be gone for 3 years. I was given a CD of Keith and Kristyn Getty songs and one of these songs was very prominent in my mind. "Speak O Lord." It's about listening to God speaking through his word so that we may become more like Jesus in "everything we do and say". It speaks about our faith increasing and there was one line that kept coming back to me.

"Help us grasp the heights of Your plans for us"

This took me right back to the verse that I had felt had been given to me by the Lord all those months ago. "I know the plans I have for you…….."

I began to meditate on the fact that the Lord had taken me right out of everything I found comfortable and put me in a place where I was fighting to understand what was going on and yet I had never felt so content with my life. It didn't make human sense. Was he going to do great things in my life? Were his plans way outside of my expectations? Time would tell.

The church was preparing for our church weekend away and Ann, Harry, Paul and I were booked in for it. It was an extremely encouraging time of Bible teaching and real friendship. The three of us, who were preparing to leave the UK, were asked to share with our church family the plans which the Charity had, for Lebanon and for Kenya. It was a great joy to share, and people were extremely encouraging. We had our flights booked and Ann and I would be leaving for Kenya directly from the weekend away venue, straight after lunch on the Sunday afternoon. Lebanon would be the destination for Harry on the Monday. We had a time of dedication by the church for the work we would be doing and then, to top it all, we sang 'Speak O Lord'. We went to the car park with our luggage and had the most amazing send off from the church family.

So the next part of our journey had begun. It had been an exciting but tiring week-end and next, Ann and I had a long overnight flight to Kenya. On arrival we were met by our dear Kenyan friends, which made us feel very much welcomed back and eager to get involved again.

3.3 Dishonesty

You will keep in perfect peace
all who trust in you,
all whose thoughts are fixed on you!
Isaiah 26:3 NLT

The new chapter of my life was about to teach me many things. Most of these lessons, I knew in theory, but they are very different when we are faced with them in reality. One thing, for certain, was not to expect the obvious. We have a Heavenly Father who can do anything, and everything, himself but chooses to use us even though we are very flawed. He wants to teach us more of himself and his expectations of us, but we don't always listen.

Ann and I arrived in Nairobi and went to the guest house for the night. The next day we went to collect the car. This was the beginning of many amazing adventures, as the car was not as I thought it would be. Unknown to me, although highly recommended and supposedly a Christian, I had bought the car from quite a crooked dealer. Although it had all the features I asked for, It clearly did not live up to how it had been described to me. However at this time, I had no idea what problems it would have. The car looked fine.

We drove the 5 hour journey back to the Home. The car did not feel right and it was difficult climbing the hills. When we reached our destination we showed the car to our driver at the Home and he was able to see immediately that nothing had been prepared for me as had been promised. He was able to identify several things that needed attention, and offered to come back to Nairobi with us to have the car properly prepared. We contacted the dealer and he agreed to rectify the problems.

I recognised that it was very easy for people to deceive me as I do trust that what people tell me is true. Here, I was a somewhat elderly and white woman, so I would have to be prepared for people to take advantage of me. I had prayed about the car and it had seemed miraculous that the very car I needed was there. He was supposedly a fellow Christian and I had believed what he said. On the plus side, owning the car taught me many things about how much the Lord was watching over and caring for me.

We made the journey back to Nairobi and our driver stayed with the vehicle to supervise the work being done. I was very grateful to him, and in fact, he looked after me and my car for many years. In the meantime, we were given a car to use for the day. We took the car with very mixed feelings because this meant that we had to drive in Nairobi, and we had not anticipated this. It was a very useful experience as the volume of traffic, and the general driving behaviour, was daunting, to say the least. We found our way around the city and took it in turns to drive. Road etiquette was greatly lacking, so if you showed the slightest sign of hesitation, people would force their way into your space. Lanes were ignored and people would cut in expecting you to hold back. You would find yourself squeezed from both sides. People would overtake on both sides of you, so you had to be very aware of everyone around you. No one stopped for red lights, so you had to go whether you wanted to or not. Because the vehicle behind was always very close it would just cause an accident if you tried to obey the lights. By the time we came back to collect my car we felt we had accomplished something that we would never have chosen to do, but had survived.

Over the next few months, in spite of his behaviour, I spent some time with the car dealer and his wife. If I was in Nairobi they would ask me to stay with them. When I needed to return to the UK I would drive to his house and stay overnight and he would drive me to the airport the next day. He would then look after the car at his house until my return, when I would collect the car and drive home. He even had extra rooms at his house and encouraged me to bring visitors there for the overnight stay, for a fee of course.

It was a year after collecting the car that it was time to renew the insurance. He called me and offered to renew the insurance for me as he had done before. I was much more confident now, and able to do more things for myself, so I said no thank you. He was very insistent but I said no. It was when I insured the car that I discovered by how much he had cheated me. I had paid far too much for the car. The car had some serious problems, and it was necessary to take it to a local mechanic who needed to take the engine out to try and identify the problem. He discovered that it had been in a very bad accident, as once the engine was removed, all the damaged bodywork was exposed. He also told me that the engine had been replaced with one that was too small for the size of the car, and that was why we struggled on the hills. Of course, we also knew by then, that it had not had 'one careful owner'!

I was very angry and called him. I told him that everything had now been revealed to me and there were only two things to be considered, either he was a very bad mechanic, or a cheat, and a liar. He profusely apologised and said that he could not return the money to me because he had spent it all. This was the answer I expected. He still wanted my friendship but I told him that in the circumstances, I felt that I could not trust him. I did stay in touch but I told him, there are consequences when we behave in a way that is dishonouring to the Lord. I think one of the saddest things is when those who give lip service to Christianity think that sin is only sin if you get caught, and that cheating is fine, if that is what you need to do to get ahead. God's blessing means that he will give you lots of money and, if

God doesn't come up with the answer you wanted, then do it your own way.

What was I to learn from all this?

I needed to pray more for wisdom because in all probability this was going to happen to me again. I did not want to become cynical and not trust anyone again. I would pray even more about the decisions I would be making in the future. The Lord makes it very clear in his word that we are all responsible before him for our actions. As nice as it would be to always have justice here and now, that may not always be possible. Ultimate justice is in the Lord's hands. I knew that to let this anger fester in me could colour my judgement in the future, and I did not want to view everybody with reservations. I realised that the outcome for this man, and others I may encounter, was best left to the Lord.

The very important lesson to learn is that God does not promise to take our problems away but he does promise to face them with us. *"I will never leave you or forsake you."* Everything I was facing was in God's control and he would bring blessing out of what seemed to be disaster, and he did. I felt at peace now and just continued with the work I had come to do.

I made another discovery during a conversation with the country Director, because it had suddenly dawned on me that when I was originally turned down for work in Africa, it had been because they were expecting a new missionary family. I asked what had happened. She told me that things didn't work out. I asked if they were still looking and she told me no. "So what will you do?" I asked. "Well we don't need to look anymore because we have you." she replied I was astonished at her reply "I am a missionary?" I exclaimed! I had never seen myself in that role. I was just me, doing a job. Now I was also reminded that I needed a long term working visa, and so, my application began. This became quite complicated as the Charity was not at this time recognised as a charity in Kenya. I had to make the application and the government would decide what kind of visa they would give me. I had all sorts of supporting documents but they did not enable me to be recognised as a missionary and so, instead, they granted me a full working visa that would cost me £2,000 for two years. Quite a shock but I decided that if God had called me, he would make this work. If it didn't work I would be going home.

3.4 Back to school and more

Learn to do good, Seek justice, Help the oppressed.
Defend the cause of orphans.
Fight for the rights of widows.
Isaiah 1:17 NLT

Ann worked with the teachers in the higher classes while I continued to work with the younger children. She remained with me for eight months, which was a real blessing. During this time we had so many good, and difficult, experiences together. I knew the time would come when she had to move on, but I was appreciating her company at this stage of the work.

The local schools' inspector came to see what was happening at our little school. We were not big enough to be registered by the government, but it was good to meet her. She was thrilled with the things being taught and said that she would like to send other teachers to see what we were doing, as we were making the curriculum work, how it was intended to. I began to understand that although the training was right, so many employers wanted things done in the 'old' way. We were invited to join in teachers seminars alongside the registered school teachers and these were very interesting and helpful days.

As we were able to add classrooms, we were also able to add more year groups to our school, and so the school was growing steadily. The classes were small so we had enough room to offer space to local children, especially those who were so poor that they could not provide the uniform required to attend the State school. We were able to provide uniforms, books and food for these children. We had a vision to raise support for 50% of our children and to offer places for 50% paying students too. The cost of the 'free' places would be covered by sponsorship. Staffing was crucial and we decided to try combining the boys from the boys home into our school and we employed the teachers from there too. However, the cost of travelling to the school every day did not prove sustainable over the years so the boys home staff eventually decided to educate their children nearer to their home. This proved to be an excellent way of building good relationships with the community. The teachers however stayed with us and we were able to employ one of them as our Head Teacher as his skills were outstanding. The school was continuing to develop well and, in agreement with the Head Teacher, I concentrated a lot of my time with the early years. It was his observation that as the children progressed through the year groups their way of learning went with them and improved the success in the other age ranges. He created a very stable environment for these children and spiritual learning and counselling were high on the agenda. It proved to be a very necessary part of their development.

We also wanted to give the teachers a wider experience, especially as we began to take in higher classes. We added classes according to the money raised to build the next classroom. We took the teachers, on a trip to Nairobi, to a school which had a very good reputation, hoping to encourage them as they began to understand new teaching methods. We also took them to see a conservation centre set up by the actress Stephanie Powers in memory of her partner William Holden. This is an amazing place where schools can visit free of charge, staying for a whole week with their children, learning about really important conservation issues. It included a visit to a nearby Animal Orphanage where the animals are cared for and reintroduced into the wild. This became a favourite place for visitors too.

As we grew, we began to reach the numbers that would require us to be registered by the government, and to take part in the all-important, year eight national exams, which we were hoping to run in our own school. The government needed us to have a minimum number of ten year eight candidates to qualify for this privilege. After we had registered, I was asked by a government official if I would drive the local officials around the area to deliver and collect exam papers. I was happy to do that but concerned that I would have to have armed guards with me. Our own home driver said that he was not happy to see me doing this, as it would be very dangerous, and so he asked permission to take my place, using my car. I was happy to agree, it felt very strange to see the school with an armed soldier at the gates during exam time. This was to prevent the school from being raided by people who wanted to steal the exam papers. I was aware of the antagonism from another local school, who did not want us to succeed, as they wanted the paying pupils for themselves and would do anything to make us fail. All the standard eight pupils were visited to entice them away from the school and drop our numbers below the required ten pupils. We persevered, the Lord blessed us and the school grew strong. Visiting teams from the USA and the UK were very encouraging in the school development, as they came to help us with special science weeks, and Vacation Bible School events during holiday time. We even had a team from the USA who came with a refurbished playground, which they set up in the school grounds, and this became very popular too. The qualified teachers who came on mission trips sometimes worked with the teachers for a few weeks at a time. This was a great encouragement to me to see the children were now being taught, in a more active way, by their Kenyan teachers. The work between the homes and the school was building up the lives of the children, many of whom had been discarded.

They were being built up in all aspects of their lives, and knowing Jesus was the basic foundation of it all.

On Sundays both homes had their own churches. They each had their own Pastors and I would visit each one on alternate Sundays. It was a good time to build friendships with the children and staff of the homes. After the service one day the pastor of the boys home asked me if I was willing to share the boy's teenage Bible study group. I accepted but, instead of sharing, I soon found myself taking it every week.

One of the most frustrating things with the Kenyan culture outside the cities was time keeping. It was so unimportant to most people and was something I had to learn how to handle. For this group of boys would stroll into the study any time that suited them, so it was difficult to make headway with consistent study. I had recently done a Bible overview at home, so I decided to make this my first project. We produced posters of our progress and put them on the wall each week. This practical activity encouraged some to arrive on time. I also noticed how much they enjoyed puzzles, like word searches, so I produced my own based on the study we would be doing. They were only allowed to do the word searches at the very beginning of our session so if anyone was late, they missed out!! Attendance after that was good and mostly on time.

As directed by the pastor, we began with teaching from the front, but I was never comfortable with that. After a couple of sessions, we put the chairs in a circle and I would encourage them to answer questions. It was slow going at first, but as we got to know each other, they were more willing to open up. I will never forget the day one of the boys told me how much he loved our study times.

I also noticed, as I was teaching the boys, that some of the women from the locality started to creep into the back of the room to listen. A few weeks later the pastor told me that the women had approached him and asked if I could teach them too, so now the work among these women began. Sunday then consisted of travelling to the boys for the Bible study, next, the morning church service followed by driving the women and their children to one of their homes where we would have lunch together followed by our study time. By now I knew that getting them to take part in a discussion would be hard. The boys were gradually opening up when they began to understand I would not be cross with them and I prayed that these women would do the same. Not many spoke fluent English but one did have good language skills and became my translator. That helped them a lot as she would ask the question, and the others would have their own little discussion, and she would come back with their answer. By the time I went home a few years later it was hard to get a word in edgeways!

Visiting their homes was a real privilege and helped me to really appreciate these women. I would meet other family members, and they welcomed me wholeheartedly. It was good to see and understand their lives. Some of them were widows and during our study times they would share how the Lord was taking care of them in hard times. Their faith in action was so good to see.

3.5 Climate

Yet the Lord longs to be gracious to you;
therefore he will rise up to show you compassion.
For the Lord is a God of justice.
Blessed are all who wait for him!
Isaiah 30:18 NIV

We were living 6,000 feet above sea level, so the climate was pleasant. It was typically about 25-30 degrees. Although so much hotter than home, it was a dry heat. We would sit on the veranda but not out in the sun. Ann and I had seen the most amazing chairs for sale, by the side of the road, on our journeys back and forth to Nairobi. The chairs were made from what looked like bamboo with a nice rounded design. We decided to buy some of these chairs, specially to use on the veranda. We discussed our top price for the chairs as we knew we would have to haggle for them. This was a new experience for us so we decided that probably about 2,000 shillings would be our absolute limit which when converted was equivalent to about £20/$30. We set off to the area where the chairs were for sale. We inspected the chairs and asked the price and we were told 400 shillings. We were so shocked that when the man saw our faces he immediately dropped the price to 300. We bought 4, a good day's sale for both us and the vendor. We also recommended them to visitors who bought some for each of the children's houses.

The weather was getting hotter and we were waiting for rain but no rain came. Our Home had a bore hole to supply us with water but it was very deep, as the water table was so much lower than our site. The lovely thing about the bore hole was that my own son and his friends had raised the money for it 5 years before, during 2002. They had visited the Home during 2002 with a large contingent from our church and it had inspired them to try and raise the money to have the borehole installed. They returned to Kenya just before Christmas of 2002 to climb Mount Kenya to raise the money through sponsorship. They made the climb with some of the older boys from the Home, and I was now living in the light of their success.

This was now turning out to be a really serious drought and the borehole was drying up. About this time the locality had started a project to bring water down from the snowcap of Mount Kenya and we were able to fill our tanks once a day to provide water for the children to drink. As the dry days continued we would scan the site to see if there were any forgotten pockets of water which we could use for washing. We scoured the site with a bucket and found a very old tank in the undergrowth which helped us for a few days. The evidence of the drought was everywhere. The electricity in Kenya is hydro-electricity and on the road to Nairobi there was a place where two rivers met and the dam produced the water needed. The rivers were so low that the iron framework was exposed.

We were using the river below our own home for laundry but it was beginning to dry up. I would drive the clothes and bedding down in the ambulance and we would use any pools of water we could find for washing. I would then drive the wet washing back to the Home to be hung out to dry. This was now getting very serious and our crops were failing for lack of water. This meant that more of the budget had to go on buying the food that we would normally have grown. The drought lasted for nine months and the relief, when the rain came, was enormous.

Rain now brought its own problems as areas of the country were flooding. Roads were washed away and villages near to rivers were destroyed. We did not suffer from flooding, as we were high up, but we did suffer from mud, which was very clingy and very slippery. Indeed, more than once I found myself flat on my face! Driving in the mud meant that I often found myself in a ditch needing help to get out, but help always came from somewhere. We would drive in the mud to town only to be delayed by huge lorries in ditches, or stranded on the road unable to move. On one occasion when a group of friends from my home church were visiting, I gave some of our teachers a lift home because the rain was so torrential. I was told that the roads had murram in them. Murram is a gravelly material, often used to surface minor roads in Africa, but it turned out not to be right. It was pitch dark, in the middle of nowhere, and I was in a ditch! I desperately tried everything I could think of to get out but to no effect. The car could barely move with inches of mud stuck to the wheels, which I was trying to scrape off with my bare hands. By now I was soaked to the skin and covered in mud from head to toe. Normally, help would just appear but not on this night. I called the home and the ambulance arrived full of young men, with the manager. He put me in the ambulance and sent me home, while they all set about rescuing the car. Everyone was very amused at the sight of me cocooned in mud!

It was times of extremes that really began to build my faith. I would feel helpless but was learning to turn to prayer straight away and the Lord never left me stranded. The prevalence in Kenya is to think that when bad things happen, we are being punished. This is such a sad view of the way God feels about us. I was able to share with our staff and children the fact that it is in the hard times when God brings us closer to him, if we will let him.

We have to hold our hands up as the human race, to acknowledge before God, that we have chosen to try and run this planet without him. He is the creator, it is his. We think we know best, but look at the mess we have made of this beautiful gift. We all live in the extremes of life, good and bad alike. God does not promise that being a Christian will solve all our problems but he does promise to always be with us in them. We have to learn to trust him no matter how extreme our circumstances are. This is faith. We are not being punished when things are difficult. Jesus has taken all our punishment on himself on the cross and we need to turn to him for forgiveness and new life. Punishment goes with rules and laws that have been broken, mercifully, that punishment has already been paid for.

Romans 3:23-25

23 For everyone has sinned; we all fall short of God's glorious standard. 24 Yet God, in his grace, freely makes us right in his sight. He did this through Christ Jesus when he freed us from the penalty for our sins. 25 For God presented Jesus as the sacrifice for sin. People are made right with God when they believe that Jesus sacrificed his life, shedding his blood.

Now we have to learn how to trust and how to look to the Lord for the answers we need. We are not forgiven by trying to be good, we are forgiven because Jesus died for us and rose again. Blessings come in many ways, through friendships, experiences and understanding and we learn to see these more and more as our relationship with God grows.

3.6 Loneliness

So do not fear, for I am with you; do not be dismayed,
for I am your God.
I will strengthen you and help you;
I will uphold you with my righteous right hand.
Isaiah 41:10 NIV

Ann continued on her journey home and I found myself alone again. Her company had been a real blessing at the start of this journey. I began to experience times of loneliness as I realised what I had left behind. I was missing out on the growing grandchildren and time with my own children. I made a yearly visit to see them all and, although we kept in touch, it was no substitute for seeing them face to face. I found myself working seven days a week as there was nowhere particular to go, and no one to go with. I had to face the anniversary of losing John on my own and I would close the curtains, and turn off my phone, to make sure that no one disturbed me in my sadness. I usually felt better the next day, but on one occasion I woke up only to find the sadness welling up in me again. I knew I had to go to the school and prayed that the Lord would help me to be able to face the day. I emailed my children and asked them to pray for me. I walked down to the school and as I went through the gate this overwhelming feeling of peace swept through me and I was fine again. I discovered later that my son in law had prayed for me just at that time and the Lord physically answered his prayer. I found, as the years went by, that this time of memories, gradually became easier for me.

I was still enjoying the work and the friendships with those around me. Then one day, I had a really nasty email from a colleague accusing me of all manner of things that were totally untrue. She obviously didn't like me, found me to be some kind of threat, and was hoping to have me sent home. I was really disturbed by this and very unsure of how to respond. All I could do was defend myself on each point in a return email. Fortunately, she had copied several other senior people into the email and, I too, had replied to 'all'. The next thing I knew was that the other people came to my defence. The whole thing was taken out of my hands and she was severely reprimanded. I was really unused to dealing with this kind of incident and could not tell what was behind such a reaction to me. It made me very wary and very aware of just how much the 'enemy' can stir things up even among God's own people. The devil wants to destroy anything that is good and we are warned in scripture in:

1 Peter 5:8 Be alert and of sober mind. Your enemy the devil prowls around like a roaring lion looking for someone to devour. 9 Resist him, standing firm in the faith, because you know that the family of believers throughout the world is undergoing the same kind of sufferings.

I don't think I had faced real opposition like this before, but this was just the beginning, and the Lord was teaching me how to handle myself, step by step. I was advised to have a mentor so that I would always have someone to talk things through with, and to pray with, and I found a good friend at home willing to listen to me whenever I needed her.

The Lord was very good to me and during my time I found team visits such a blessing as I could talk freely and people would understand me! It was lovely to enjoy people with a similar sense of humour and I also had the opportunity to travel with them on Safari. Two other young colleagues came and worked alongside me for a while, giving me the company I needed from time to time.

3.7 Time out

Fear of man will prove to be a snare,
but whoever trusts in the Lord is kept safe.
Proverbs 29:25 NIV

I was missing my family very much and as, Christmas was approaching, I decided this would be a good time to go home and see them. Adam was finishing Primary School, so, in consultation with his home manager, we decided that this was a good time to take him to meet the rest of my family. It seemed a good idea to include the home manager, Damian, in this visit as it could be quite hard for Adam to be so far from everything he knew. We began by getting permission from his mother to take him on the visit. She agreed and signed the necessary paperwork. We then approached the Children's Office to get permission from them. The local office was very happy for him to travel and referred us to the larger office in the next town. They too agreed it would be a very good experience for him and referred us, with a recommendation, to the main Children's Office in Nairobi. We waited for the answer and were very shocked when we got a negative reply. No explanation just NO. This annoyed me and I learned from staff members that there were people working in the Children's Office who hated the Charity and would block anything we applied for. This had occurred because of historic issues, but it was a constant nuisance. I decided that if the Lord was in favour of this visit, I would go to Nairobi to face these people and see what they would say face to face.

I went with Adam, Damian, and a representative from our main office and we presented ourselves to them. I explained about the application to travel and asked to see a senior member of staff. There was a real sense of shock that we had done this and they tried to stall our visit. They went for advice from someone in a higher position and returned to tell us that the Chief Children's Officer was in a meeting and not expected back until after lunchtime. I told them we would wait and to please show us where his office was so that we could wait there. I could see that they didn't expect us to wait, but they had no choice. We sat outside the office for a couple of hours and at last the Chief Children's Officer appeared. He looked at us with a bewildered expression and asked "What are you doing here?" I told him about the planned visit and the refusal from his office for us to travel. He asked, "Do you have the mother's permission?" "Yes." "Does he have a passport?" "Yes." "Does he have a visa?" "Not yet because we have to have your permission first." "Well go and travel and enjoy yourselves." So armed with his permission we made our way to the British Visa Office.

We were on cloud nine and hurried back into Nairobi. We needed photos for the visas so we parked in a familiar carpark and I sat in the car with our office rep while Damian and Adam went off to have the photos taken. I was so relaxed now that I had stopped being vigilant and someone spoke to me through the window of the car. As I turned, another man on the other side of the vehicle put his hand through the open window and snatched my bag, which contained all the official papers for the visa application,18,000 shillings to pay for everything and my own personal papers and cash.

I could not believe it and leapt out of the car to chase the culprit but I could not see anyone running and hadn't seen their face to recognise them. People around became aware that something was happening and they surrounded me asking if they could help. Some ran in different directions to see if they could spot anyone with the bag. Then suddenly I saw a man coming from between two parked cars, with a carrier bag poking out of which, I could see, was the handle of my bag. I shouted, "That's my bag" and ran as fast as I could to catch him. I must have looked quite fierce because he threw the bag to one side and just ran as fast as he could. Someone was apprehended but I could not, in all honesty, identify him as the man I had seen, so he had to be let go. When I looked in the bag, all the official papers were gone so I said, "He has stolen all my papers!!" Suddenly someone cried out "Here they are, he threw them under the car." When I checked everything not one thing was missing. It was such an astonishing event that we had a lovely round of applause and a great many people were praising the Lord for helping us. They told me that no one ever got anything back from robberies in Nairobi so, it must have been the hand of God taking care of me.

I got back to the car and found our rep from the office, sitting in the driver's seat. In my haste to catch the thief I had left the car with the keys in the ignition. He told me that another ploy for stealing cars was for the would be thieves to create an incident to distract the driver, so that he/she would leave the keys in the ignition and then they would just drive away with the car. I never forgot this and on another day when I found myself in exactly that position, while I investigated the incident I locked my car and kept the keys with me. The men who had caused the diversion laughed and acknowledged that I had beaten them.

Adam and Damian got back to the car unaware of all the drama that had taken place. We drove on to the visa office to submit our application but the dramatic events of the day had not finished yet!

We went to the desk for submitting all the paperwork for our visa applications, praying that we had everything we needed. The person behind the desk was very encouraging and wanted to be sure that Adam would have this once in a lifetime experience. We went through the whole process and she asked for proof that he would be returning to go to high school. We needed a letter from the Head Teacher confirming this, but we had none because he was finishing primary school and did not yet have a place in high school. I was so deflated, after all we had been through that day to then fall at the last hurdle seemed cruel. Suddenly Damian said "Can I sign anything to show that this is true as I am his home manager." Her eyes lit up and she dictated a letter for him to sign confirming that he would be returning, and that then they would be looking for a high school. Having submitted everything, we went back to the guest house exhausted, certain that the Lord's hand had been on everything. Now all we could do was wait for the visas to arrive.

I was so certain that the Lord was saying yes to our trip that I went ahead and booked the flights. With just a few days to go we had the green light so another trip to Nairobi was now needed to collect the papers. As it was Friday, and our journey was the following Tuesday, it was now or never but I needed the home manager with me to sign for the visas. I sent him a message and asked him to meet me in Nairobi but I was really concerned that he may not make it in time before the office closed. Again, the Lord opened the way for him. He had gone to wait for a matatu. A matau is like a mini bus, the public transport throughout Kenya. This was the the only way he could make the journey, but it would be slow with all the stops on the way. As he was waiting, a matatu pulled up but it was not the usual one. This one had been hired privately and was going to drive straight to Nairobi. He asked if he could have a lift and the man said yes. Another amazing answer to prayer.

A whirlwind of experiences that proved yet again that God was in control and the enemy could not defeat his plans.

When we returned from the trip, three weeks later, we had a message to say that the Children's Office had withdrawn their consent for Adam's journey. I didn't want any comeback because we had taken the trip without their written consent so we went to our local Children's office to prove that he had returned. The lady was very bemused by the whole incident of refusal. She asked him questions about his trip and told him she was very pleased that he had enjoyed it so much. We never heard another thing about it.

3.8 Home

29 "Yes," Jesus replied, "and I assure you that everyone who has given up house or brothers or sisters or mother or father or children or property, for my sake and for the Good News, 30 will receive now in return a hundred times as many houses, brothers, sisters, mothers, children, and property—along with persecution. And in the world to come that person will have eternal life.
Mark 10:29-30 NLT

The time back at home was filled with great joy but was also a stark reminder of what I had left behind. Adam had a great time with my family and with friends. It was a very good experience for him as I wanted him to meet them and for them to get to know him. In the back of my mind was the fact that if anything happened to me they would continue with his sponsorship until he was old enough to leave the home. Damian was able to visit his family in the UK, before he returned, and Adam and I had the last week on our own.

Before we came back to Kenya I found the verses in Mark 10:29-30 (above) and really felt that it was a picture of my life at this moment. I was experiencing the truth of these words as I had more than a hundred children and even adults who all called me Mum. I had somewhere to live and a busy life learning a vast amount about God's promises and how to trust him. My family at home were extremely precious to me but I had been asked to leave them behind, to work among people who were becoming another family to me. My own family, now grown, were settled into their lives and the new family were so vulnerable living lives filled with such uncertainty.

- I had to learn that commitment was costly, leaving my family so far away but God is in control. I had to leave my home in the care of others, thankfully, they were proving to be such good stewards;

- I had to face the fact that I was vulnerable in this new culture because I was seen as an easy target, and learn to trust God in all circumstances.

- I had never really faced situations where people behaved in such a personally antisocial way before and I was learning how to confront these issues.

The one thing that really struck me about the verses above (Mark 10:29-30) was the statement "along with persecution." I had tasted a little already but had no idea of the persecution I would be facing in the near future.

4. Learning how to trust and rely on God

4.1 Three new homes

36 For everything comes from him and exists by his
power and is intended for his glory.
All glory to him forever! Amen.
Romans 11:36 NLT

Over the next few months, we gained three more homes. These homes had been attached to the Charity before, but they had withdrawn and had decided to work independently. This had not gone well for any of them so they were reattached, and each one was given new staff. I had a conversation with the director and I was asked to visit each of these new homes.

I began in the east of Kenya and driving there was a challenge because of the very dusty roads. This was a very different place, high in the hills, with beautiful views. The home was small with just ten children who attended the local school, which was just a few yards away. I went to see the school, which was a good school and the children were doing well.

The very youngest children were in a nursery class held in the home itself and the teacher wanted help to make sure she was providing the right learning experiences for the children. This class was in a room big enough to accommodate local children too and we had a delightful couple of weeks looking at the curriculum, making posters and some simple activities. A young man, who was a pupil in a local high school, would come in after school to help the older children with their homework and this was delightful to see. He lived very close by, with his grandmother, having lost both of his parents.

I met the head teacher of another, much bigger, local school who was very supportive to the home and he took me to see his school where he asked me to pray with the standard eight children as they would soon be taking their final exams and the results would affect their future. He took me into each classroom and I met the staff and some of the children. When we emerged from the last classroom I was confronted with the whole school waiting to hear from me. This was to become a recurring theme throughout my years in Kenya and I had to learn how to speak to both adults and children with no preparation on both general topics and Bible messages. They were lovely children and I told them where I was from and then encouraged them to ask questions. This was such a good time and I was able to excite them, by telling them about other parts of the world, and to encourage them in their studies.

The children from the home would take me for walks around their community where I saw some really heart wrenching situations. For example we came across two small children, one who was four years old holding a baby of 9 months. The mother was working, as her husband had died and she had no option but to work so that she could care for her children. She would leave the children on their own, and her neighbours would keep an eye on them while they went about their own daily duties. We often found that the small communities would care, as best they could, for the desperate people within them. This was another clear indication to me, that where there were physical needs we had to understand the culture before deciding what we would do. One example of this was in this particular home. We had a borehole with access to clean water, and the whole locality was able to benefit from this. The only other access to water, for locals, was to walk down to the river and carry it back in containers for their daily needs. People would give a few shillings to the home, towards the maintenance of the borehole.

I then went to visit the second home, which was in the west of Kenya, with the vice president of the Charity and some visitors. On this occasion we flew from Nairobi to Kisumu where we were met by one of the staff of the home. We then drove to the village near the home. It was difficult to actually reach the home as the track was narrow, and rough and very muddy when it had rained. I did get stuck there on one visit as I drove across what looked like a green field but which turned out to be a swamp! The local people came to my rescue and eventually my car was towed back onto drier land. There were plans to build a new road, taking a different route, but it needed bridges over local rivers and this took a lot of time. The community were looking forward to a new road, as in the rainy season, the rivers would swell and become almost impassable. It was also very dangerous for the children on their way to school, as this home was literally on the banks of Lake Victoria. The community was very dependent on the lake and there were many fishing boats here, so the children took some of our party out on the lake where they saw hippos. With such close proximity to the lake there were, equally benefits and difficulties. One of the benefits was the delicious meals of fresh tilapia, a fish I had never tasted before, and eating it was a great experience. One of the difficulties was, that in the rainy season, the water of the lake would flood onto the site and although many measures were taken to keep the water out of the buildings, it was a losing battle. During these times the children and staff would suffer from both malaria and typhoid. On one occasion on leaving the home rather late in the evening we became aware of some large, dark shapes around us. Then we realised we were surrounded by hippos which were walking back to the lake, we stayed still until they disappeared among the trees. This had been quite an awesome sight. We could not stay onsite, as the home was small, so we stayed in a nearby guest house. Our visit was a good one, getting to know the children and staff but, there were so many different problems here that would need to be considered if this home were to remain open.

The third home was also in the west, high up in the hills with beautiful views, but the site was also on a very steep incline from one end to the other. We travelled across the Rift Valley and came to the town called Kisii, a place heaving with people, which had an amazing market. We stayed at an hotel there as we could not reach the home in one day. The following morning, we travelled for another 26 kilometres to the place where the tarmac road came to an end. The rest of the journey took an hour on very rough dirt roads, where potholes and ruts were so deep, that it felt quite precarious, as we made our way to the gates. We entered the home, where we met the staff and children, Here as usual the children all attended local schools within walking distance of the home. The buildings were all clustered together in one place, as the site was so steep with the lower part of the site being reserved for children's physical activities. To the right, looking down on the site they were also growing their own food supported by a borehole for water. Every morning the children would go to the borehole with water containers, pump the water up by hand and carry their full containers to the kitchen for the day's supply of water. We stayed until after dark, as it was always dark somewhere between 6.00 - 7.00pm, and then they would light the kerosene lamps for the evening. These lamps enabled them to eat their meals together and then to do their homework before going to bed. On later visits, I was able to visit the local schools where I was, once again, asked to pray for the children who would be taking their standard eight exams. These exams were so very important to the children as it would determine their eligibility for high school. This was a lovely home with dedicated staff who showed a real love for the children.

It was an education for me to see just how these children lived, to become aware of and understand their communities, to be faced with the inequalities in this world, and to see the good and the bad in human nature. I had so much more than these people, so it became even more important to listen to the Lord's voice and to know when and how to give.

Having now visited all the homes I was about to be introduced to another area in which I was to become involved.

4.2 High School

Do not worry about how you will defend
yourselves or what you will say,
12 for the Holy Spirit will teach you at
that time what you should say."
Luke 12:11b-12

I was not needed as often in school on a daily basis, so I now provided teacher training sessions and visits, to keep monitoring the progress of the development of the school.

I found myself drawn into other areas of work and I was invited to visit the high schools and vocational schools where our older children were now living. A generous donor had made it possible for some of our children to attend these boarding schools. The school system after standard eight was high school or vocational school dependent on the grade of the final standard eight exams. There was a local day high school but people would look down on this as inferior to the boarding system. The desire was always to get the children into a boarding school, as the best option, but it also brought many challenges to light.

We began a tour of each of these schools and I came away with very mixed feelings about this form of education.

The children, who were away at school only returned home during each holiday and I was concerned about the lack of contact with them. To see the students during term time, would be at the discretion of the Head Teacher. The students were accommodated in large dormitories and all the schools provided basic care. Some of the schools were very harsh in their dealings with the children and children from a children's home were often considered to be less important. I had to learn restraint in what I said, and the way I said it, as there could be consequences for the children involved. It was a real joy to see when an individual child was recognised for their contribution to the school, and we did have some shining examples where they were chosen for trusted positions.

Some were very well monitored during leisure time, others were not, and the young people were introduced to bad influences. Unfortunately, a trend began to develop, in high schools all over the country, where the students would cause real damage in the school in the hopes of being sent home or making it impossible to take their exams. Many young people were expelled at this time. High school was for four years and these rebellions usually took place in year three. There were some very sad incidents with students dying as a result of fires.

The government intervened to try and control the rebellious incidents by making the consequences severe. Cheating during exam time was a real problem in some of the schools, so the government response, when a culprit was discovered, was to downgrade all the students in the class. This was such a disappointment to all the students who had worked so hard, and in one case, the results of the class were completely wiped out so the students had to take the whole year again, if they wanted to get any kind of result. The following year, because of exam fraud suspicions, they were again downgraded, which sadly removed the chance of going to university for one of our students. He could not face taking the year for a third time.

I loved making these visits, and my understanding of the system, and my insight into the good and bad aspects of it, were really helpful. I was always greeted with enthusiasm and it was on these occasions I would be asked to "address" the pupils in large assemblies at a moment's notice. Sometimes, this involved a brief greeting but could also involve a short bible message. I never knew what was coming, but God in his wisdom always gave me the words to say. This is when I knew the words of Jesus in Luke 12 (quoted at the beginning of this section) to be so very true.

I began to be invited, along with other staff to attend special school events, such as prize givings, which enabled us to spend time with our young people over a picnic lunch. We would watch displays given by the students and be allowed to go on a tour of the school. On one such occasion I was privileged to take the place of a parent, as the students were often asked to bring a parent forward, as they received their prize. Although I was known as "Mum" to all our children, this was the first time I had realised how important it was to some of our children to have the support of a parent at these public occasions.

It was very hard when I could see an injustice in the way our young people were treated and although I tried to intervene on several occasions, I was respectfully listened to and tolerated as I had my say, but rarely given the benefit of the doubt. On one occasion, Adam, my own sponsor child had been accused of bullying, had been suspended and was sent home to me. I had a long conversation with him to ascertain the truth of the allegations and I was convinced he was wrongly accused but had no idea how we could prove this. We were called back to the school for a meeting with a senior staff member, and much to my relief, the boy who had been bullied testified to the fact that Adam was the one who had defended him against the bullies. We were just coming to the end of the meeting, which had decided no further action was to be taken against Adam, when the Head Teacher came striding into the meeting declaring that Adam was guilty and was going to be punished. He would not listen to anyone, not even the victim. As they led Adam from the room, he looked at me and said, "It's ok Mum." I was devastated but helpless and just prayed that he would be able to withstand the punishment which I knew would be a severe beating. So many children had to bear, and quietly accept, injustice, especially the most vulnerable who had no one to defend them.

This was all replicated in the girls home as I would be called to the schools to discuss progress or other issues that had arisen and open day visits were very encouraging. I had face to face meetings with heads, deputy heads and classroom teachers, when I was able to discuss issues and find solutions that we could act on together. Behaviour issues were always very complex, since some of the behaviour stemmed from long term abuse as they were growing up before they came to the home. It was always a joy to work with staff who understood the background of the girls in their care, could see their potential, and gave them every encouragement to succeed.

The children who did not reach the exam level to qualify them for a place in high school would be sent to board at a vocational school. This was such a good route for many of our children as it would give them skills that would lead to employment. There was a wide variety of skills on offer and I would visit these schools to see which ones had the best courses for our children. Unfortunately this was seen as a lesser route than high school for the children, but for me, it was such a good way to train the children to be able to care for themselves after they left the home. I was concerned for the children who left high school with only lower academic qualifications, and who therefore, found it hard to find work as opportunities seemed limited.

Supporters of these young people began to ask questions about further education for the young person they were supporting, and this led me to look at the requirements for entry into colleges and universities. I also went to visit the young men who were already in college to see how they were progressing. The biggest problem was the living conditions, which varied greatly.

This needed lots of prayer and advice from my Kenyan colleagues as I familiarised myself with the process of further education.

I began to look at the lives of the young people who had left the home to see how they were coping with life outside. I noticed that in the past a young man who had gone to work in a garage had been given the tools that he would need as a parting gift. Another young man had gone to work in a local boarding primary school, as an unqualified teacher, where the pay was low but he had been given accommodation and food. It made me think about the next step for all our children. This was just the beginning of their independent lives and it seemed tough that they should have to step out into the world with no particular support. I also noticed that some of them were still living in the home, as they had nowhere else to go. They needed some kind of support to take these first steps into adult life. So they were encouraged to look for local employment that would give them enough for rent and basic food. The unqualified teaching work, in the private schools, helped several of them and others took employment in the local town in shops or other outlets and hotels. Some of them were very inventive in the way they chose to earn money!

Philip began by working in a private school and then moved on to work for a man running a 'money booth'. This was for mobile money, 'mpesa', which people would use to transfer money to each other by their mobile phones. If you needed to put money in, or take money out, you would use one of these booths. Philip's dream was to go to university to study Business Administration, so he worked hard and saved what he could. His savings grew, and he took out a loan to buy a motorbike. He employed a young man to ride the motorbike for him as a taxi. The young man had to bring a set amount to Philip daily, and the balance would be his own as his wages. This arrangement allowed Philip to pay off the loan and still save. After a couple of years, we were able to find Philip a place in the local university. By now his ambition had changed, as he had observed that many students were taking Business Administration and jobs were becoming scarce. He chose to study procurement, as he saw that all businesses needed procurement. By now he had managed to buy another motorbike for himself. The morning would be spent using his motorbike as a taxi, the afternoon was study time, with lectures in the evening, so that all through his time in college he was able to earn enough money for his basic needs. On gaining his degree, he went straight into full-time employment.

4.3 College

"Physical training is good, but training for
godliness is much better,
promising benefits in this life and in the life to come."
1 Timothy 4:8 NLT

Working with the home managers, we began to place young people in colleges as opportunities arose. I loved visiting these colleges and encouraging our students as well as gaining more and more insight into the best places for them.

We found that sponsors were very keen to take part in this and, at this time, we were able to place those students with the right qualifications into university. We made the best use we could of the education schemes in Kenya, where the government would pay for tuition, and we would pay for living expenses. We were also blessed in being able to use the support schemes from the US, so we would apply for as many of these as we could . These schemes also enabled helping some of our staff to complete college courses.

I then decided that there needed to be some kind of training before leaving the home to help equip these young people as they began to face the world outside. We wanted, above everything else, to encourage them in their Christian walk and up to this point we had no real idea how they were doing. We had thirty young people who had moved on from the homes and it was decided to bring all thirty of them back to the home for a week's conference. We developed a programme that would look at each aspect of our lives based on scripture and the Lord's expectations for us as his children.

I asked various members of staff to prepare talks for them, as well as those I would be taking. We accommodated them in the team bungalow where they cooked for themselves and worked out their own rotas for cleaning etc. We would also spend time with them in the evenings and it was great to see them enjoying these social times as they spent time together sharing their experiences. They were very excited to see each other and expressed their desire to do this again as they had enjoyed seeing each other so much. We would love to have been able to do this for them but we did not have the resources to repeat the experience. However, they were then encouraged to develop an alumni group of male and female young people who had left the homes and were now young adults. We went through the process of officially creating it with them. We hoped that this would be a good way for them to stay in touch with each other. This training became an annual event for all our children when they reached the age for leaving the homes.

I would spend time scouring brochures, visiting various colleges and making plans to find the most suitable courses. This entailed a lot of travelling and staying in various parts of the country, which became quite complicated as we had to find cheap accommodation. I always made sure I had a few students with me, at any time, as a white woman on her own would be quite vulnerable. All of these journeys were in my old, troublesome car so we prayed before each journey and, although we always prayed for safety, we also learned to pray for God to walk with us through the day. God had not promised a trouble free life so we needed to ask him to make us aware of his presence no matter what we had to face. The more we saw God's hand in our travels, the more we trusted that no matter what, he would be there helping with our decisions and their consequences.

If we had a puncture it was important to change the wheel immediately and then find the nearest garage to have the puncture mended. We had some regular petrol stations, where we would refuel, and we made some good friends with the people who worked there, because of our regular visits. In fact I once pulled into a new garage, on the road near to Nairobi, only to be greeted by the young man at the petrol pump, with "Hello Madam Ruth." I had never seen this young man before but I discovered he had lived in our local village and went to school with some of our boys. This became a regular place to refuel. The boys and I travelled to a town called Kisumu, on the banks of Lake Victoria. It was a beautiful place with wonderful views from the hotel, but this journey had taken us many hours and my handbrake had failed, so I needed a mechanic to look at the car for me before the return journey. The hotel recommended a garage and the mechanic collected the car. I asked him to check the brakes for me as well as the handbrake, as I had become aware of some inconsistencies when using the brakes on this journey.

We walked around the town absorbing all the sights. We explored a bustling market selling fruit, vegetables, clothes, shoes and many other household goods. Then we visited the college where one of my students was in attendance, so I was able to have a good conversation with the principal discussing the student's progress. The students I'd brought with me had not yet started courses, so this was a good way to help them experience life outside their own villages and to learn about other parts of the country. After my meeting we walked to the place where the student was renting a room, which he proudly showed to us. We had a good day together and, having arranged to pick up the car first thing the next day, we went to bed. Next morning we met the mechanic who explained the completed work and then we started our return journey.

After about one hour of driving, my brakes failed completely. I had no hand brake and no main brakes! I was approaching a line of stationary traffic so pulled off the road as soon as possible and drifted to a stop. I found someone who claimed to know about cars and asked him to look at the brakes for me. I also called the mechanic who had done the work. He was horrified to hear what had happened and he spoke to the man who was now looking at the problem. The two men talked with one another and in half an hour the brakes were working again. We continued our journey with much prayer. Within another thirty minutes the brakes had failed again. I decided at this point that we would see how far we could get using the gears to slow us down. It is not always safe to stop in places that are unfamiliar, as anything could happen, so we limped our way home. Normally, we would have been stopped several times by the police but on this occasion, just when we needed it, we did not see any policemen or roadblocks. The journey took ten hours but, with carefully controlling the speed, we managed to reach home. I was so relieved to be home I forgot to slow down enough as we approached the gates of the home and smashed my way through. The poor guards thought they were being attacked but I shouted that it was "only me" and they came out of hiding. The dent in the gates was a constant reminder of that journey!

This experience was yet again one where God was showing me how much he was looking after me. We had had no alternative but to trust him to get us home safely as it was too dangerous to stop in the dark. I had never known a journey where I was not stopped by the police and yet, on this night, there was none to be seen. As I said, at the beginning, we had learned to pray that the Lord would walk with us no matter what happened. So, his words, "*Never will I leave you; never will I forsake you.*" Hebrews 13:5 NIV took on a new significance for me. I felt I had experienced the same level of God's recognition as expressed in Matthew 10:29-31

29 Are not two sparrows sold for a penny? Yet not one of them will fall to the ground outside your Father's care. 30 And even the very hairs of your head are all numbered. 31 So don't be afraid; you are worth more than many sparrows.

4.4 Students

Whatever you do, work at it with all your heart,
as working for the Lord, not for human masters,
Colossians 3:23 NIV

These were such exciting days with the Lord showing me over and over again how much he was caring for me.

Some of the young people had not seen other family members for years so, where possible, we would give them the opportunity to revisit their original homes before starting their college courses. One such visit was in the west of Kenya, to a place just outside the town of Kisii. The journey was long, so we stayed overnight in a small hotel, and reached the family home the next day. The reunion between the brothers was a joy to see as they had lost both their parents and had been taken in by an aunt. When the children came to her, she was struggling to care for them and her own family, so the older two boys came to our home and the youngest brother was taken in by another similar organisation. She was a good aunt, protecting the family home, and always keeping in touch with them. Hospitality is so important in Kenya and the aunt wanted to offer us a meal so, despite having another boy to meet later, we accepted the offer. When the meal was over, and we were able to say goodbye, to the family we continued with our journey.

We went through the town and by now it was beginning to get dark but unfortunately we had about another two hours of driving ahead of us. As usual my hand brake had failed but we were managing all right until we turned onto a steep upward hill where my engine literally just died. Had my battery failed? There had been no warning lights to say we had a problem.

The one thing that was so good about these long journeys was that the boys could see with their own eyes that God was taking care of us. I could not put the handbrake on so I had to put it into first gear to hold the car from rolling back down the hill. We prayed for the Lord's help and then I asked the boys to approach a large crowd of people who were waiting for a matatu and ask if there was anyone there who knew anything about cars. A man stepped from the crowd and said "Yes. I work at the garage at the bottom of the hill and my speciality is electrics." Why was I not surprised!! He got the car moving and we drove to his garage where he could fix the problem and make a thorough inspection of the electrics, ensuring that we would make it to our destination. Another useful friend who had helped in our hour of need! From then on the car performed perfectly and we met the other boy who had been patiently waiting for us for three hours!

There were many aspects of the courses and work experiences that were interesting. We had a young man, Simon, at college studying hospitality and tourism and he was doing very well on the course but needed a work experience placement for the next part of his tourism course. It was hard to see how we could help him find the placement and, as I was due to go home, there was nothing that I could do at that moment. Having reached my home in the UK, I was spending some time with the two young ladies who were now my house-sitters. It was then that I discovered that one of them had been born in Kenya and still had a sister there. Can you guess? She managed a large tourism business, which catered for the needs of the UN in Nairobi. So she contacted her sister and between us we managed eventually to get the two of them to meet. Simon was given the work experience and they were so impressed with his work ethic and performance, that he was offered a job as soon as he had finished his course. He has continued to perform well and has a good position in the company. Another very clear provision of our Heavenly Father caring for his children. Simon is also well established in his local church, serving among the young people.

Sometimes events took us completely by surprise. I found myself with one young man, Joel, who had been looking at the engineering course in the main Nairobi university. As they always took the cream of the students for these courses, they became full very quickly. We decided to just look at the engineering department, even though we had no intention of applying yet. All applications were in and even the late applications had been completed. We found our way to the dean's office, just to see if we could talk with him and see what would be required for the next intake and if there would be any possibility of Joel qualifying for a place. We reached his secretary's office and began to chat with her but she was very puzzled by me, being white, and acting like his parent. She then, of course, discovered that Joel had grown up in a children's home and she asked us to wait while she spoke to the dean. We entered the dean's office and he began to ask many questions about Joel and his background. He then said directly to him, "I want you on my course and I want you now!" We were shocked, as he picked up the phone and told someone on the other end that they were to make room for this young man even though all applications were finished. He then asked me to write a letter of recommendation and we were told to go and find out from the secretary all that needed to be done. We had about five days to complete everything, including finding him somewhere to live and to organise all the finances. He had wonderful sponsors who were eager to help and so, his five year course began. Each year there would be a cull of students who did not make the grade in that year's exams and Joel always made the grade. Having completed his degree, Joel is now working with a friend in the solar heating business, as well as running a shop for organic food with his wife, working for an engineering firm, and doing engineering drawings as and when required. He is always looking for further ways to develop his experiences. He has such a strong faith and has always seen and acknowledged the Lord's hand on his life.

There was also a young lady who many would have not considered as being worth much. Her high school results were not too good but the manager of the home had great faith in her abilities, so we went together to a catering college where her qualifications for the course only let her in at the very basic level. After a lot of persuasion from the home manager they let her start at the level above, on the understanding that if she could not cope they would take her back down. We agreed to this and she started on the course performing extremely well. The college always spoke so highly of her whenever I went to visit and her placement at the Safari Lodge in Amboselli game park proved how good she was. After qualifying she took a job in a hotel at the equator where she rose, from being in the kitchen, to managing all the housekeeping. Her real dream was to have an industrial oven of her own and to bake. Sadly after a very difficult time she found herself in need of work and the donations from my UK church enabled her to buy the oven of her dreams and begin baking. However, then the pandemic hit and it was hard for her to make a living but she was able to get a job in the local hospital, so she would bake early in the morning and take her goods to the hospital to sell. She now has a piece of land where she is getting ready to build her house. She has a clear and strong faith and she knows that none of this could have happened without the Lord being in it with her. These are just a few examples of the Lord guiding the steps of the young people who had lived in the homes. We have seen so many move forward in their lives and we give all praise to the Lord as we see these young people growing in their faith and living their lives to glorify God.

4.5 Teaching Women

It is the same with my word.
I send it out, and it always produces fruit.
It will accomplish all I want it to,
and it will prosper everywhere I send it.
Isaiah 55:11 NLT

The Charity made sure our senior staff were kept up to date with training and this would take place in any of the homes, sometimes it would involve people from the States and the UK. They were really good sessions with excellent teaching which also gave us a good opportunity to get to know each other better. This training would usually be for about a week and our shared accommodation meant that we would have evenings together giving us time to chat.

On one such occasion I was in a vehicle with various members of staff and was told about a women's conference that was being planned in the west of Kenya. I was then asked if I would like to attend. I liked the idea of going to the conference as it would be very interesting to see how these women were being taught, so I agreed and much to my astonishment, I was told, "I think we can get you about 100 women." "You mean I am the speaker for this conference?" I exclaimed. "Yes of course" came the reply.

I had walked right into that one!! I had never done anything like this before and they were now chatting about suitable dates so we went ahead and organised the conference, which I then discovered would be held over two days. As I began to think about a subject for the conference I decided to look at what the bible says about women in all aspects of life. However, I needed time to prepare for two days of talks, and this whole thing was very daunting. Also, I needed somewhere quiet to think, and to give myself time to prepare thoroughly, so I decided to spend two nights at the Aberdare Country Club where I knew I could have a room in the grounds to myself, with no one to disturb me.

I duly arrived and found that there were very few visitors. Most of the people arriving came for lunch, followed by a Safari tour and a night at 'the Ark'. That evening, I was to have my evening meal in my room, but there was a power cut, so I had to have a candlelit dinner in the main restaurant and I ended up spending the evening with the owner who was doing the same. It was a lovely evening but it considerably reduced my study time. They were extremely attentive for the time I was there, frequently checking up to see if I had everything I needed and offering me cups of tea and food, I felt it was not quite the space and quiet I had been looking for, but I really appreciated their efforts.

The time for the conference arrived and I drove to the west of Kenya. I took the opportunity to take some students with me so that they could have my car, while I was with the women, so this would enable them to visit some of their friends who had moved back to this area. We stayed at a familiar guest house and drove to the venue in the morning where I was amazed to see that we had almost 100 women who had come to hear God's Word, and they apologised that the numbers were low! I was also surprised to see a bishop and seven pastors who also had decided to attend. I had thought this was a women's conference!! A lady had been appointed to interpret for me, and so we began the day's teaching. Lunch was provided and we sat outside under the trees to eat together. The bishop approached me and was complimentary about my teaching. At the end of the first day a lady stood up to say thank you for the day's teaching, but she also announced that the men would not be welcome to participate the following day, and that they would have to sit outside under the trees for the day. This conference was for women and they needed their privacy. A big round of applause followed.

I was feeling anxious now, about the second day's teaching, as I was entering the area where I felt under prepared. I rang my mentor in the UK so that she could pray with me. We had a good talk about the next day's programme and how I might approach it. She reminded me of the scripture where Jesus told his disciples not to worry about times when they had to speak up for their faith and he told them that they would be given the words. I needed to commit the whole day to the Lord and ask the Holy Spirit to use me to say what he wanted me to say rather than just rely on my preparation. He was the one who knew the hearts of the people who would be listening so he would know what they needed to hear.

I went to bed having committed everything to the Lord. The next day I drove to the venue, said goodbye to the boys and began to unpack my bag. To my horror I had left the actual notes for the day's teaching back at the guest house and only had the pictures to illustrate the talk with me. I had no way of getting to my notes so now I had to face the whole day and learn what it really meant to rely on the Lord for everything. This day was incredibly different from how yesterday had been! Without the presence of the men, the ladies began to open up and we had the most wonderful day exploring scripture together, with them freely asking and answering questions. These ladies had quite a mixture of circumstances. There were a few who were conventionally married, some were second or third wives, some were living in abusive relationships, and some were widowed. Their family lives were so different from anything I had ever known.

I had one young woman who stood up and told us, "My daughter got sent home from school recently for some kind of bad behaviour, so I beat her. The next day I told her to go back to school but she refused, so I beat her again. After several beatings she eventually returned to school. Now you are telling me I should have talked with my daughter to find out what had happened before taking action." I had been teaching them about family relationships at this point. I told her, "Yes, you needed to establish whether the punishment was deserved or not and then talked about resolving the situation." As I have said before, my own experience of Kenyan schools was that children could be punished unfairly and not allowed to have a say. It was not always possible to get a just solution but at least she could support her daughter, rather than punish her a second time. "When I go home today I am going to talk to my daughter to find out why she was sent home," was the response. I prayed that she and her daughter would be able to build a closer relationship.

God proved to me that day that he really means what he says. He was in control. He was guiding me and his words were being heard. I felt very encouraged and I was sure that these women had heard his voice and not what I had assumed they needed. It is a lesson that I have never forgotten.

Trusting God in these circumstances had been quite a lesson.

- Acknowledging the need to ask God to walk with me through the day.

- Depending on God to keep me physically safe.

- Relying on the Holy Spirit to guide my speaking

- Understanding that God really means what he says.

5. Learning how much God cares for me

5.1 Community

16 Live in harmony with each other.
Don't be too proud to enjoy the company
of ordinary people.
And don't think you know it all!
Romans 12:16 NLT

It was very important to build relationships with local people. As I have previously indicated I often visited the nearest safari lodge called The Aberdare Country Club. The manager, at that time, already had a good relationship with the children's homes as his own daughter had worked there for a while. They encouraged us to bring the older children to dance and sing Christmas songs and carols every Christmas Eve for all their visitors. A bus would come to the home for the children and they would perform outside under the stars, sometimes late into the night. It was a beautiful occasion, always appreciated, and the children would be given a candlelit meal on the veranda. We would then be taken home in the bus with a generous donation of 10,000 shillings (Approx £100 / $135 at that time).

I approached the manager to see if they would allow me to bring groups of children to the Country Club for a swim on a Saturday afternoon. I offered to pay for the privilege but he would not hear of it, so I took 6-8 children each week and they really enjoyed swimming or paddling. Over a period of months, I managed to take all the children from the two homes and we were treated with great respect. I was however concerned at one point that they may not want these children there when the place was full of visitors but in fact it was quite the opposite. If there were visitors, the children were introduced by the manager and we were treated like royalty, especially by the Kenyan visitors.

I was approached by one of our own young men, Jacob, who asked me to take him to the Country Club, where he was going to ask for a job. When we arrived, I went to greet the staff members, who had become good friends, and then sat on the veranda to watch the animals. There were peacocks, various deer and warthogs that came close to the building and in the distance we often saw giraffes, zebras and eland. Jacob had an interview with the Manager but unfortunately there were no actual jobs, although they were, however, able to offer him experience, board and lodging but without pay. He decided to accept and was able to work in every department. He became very popular among the staff and even developed some ideas to promote the staff in the Lodge, taking photographs and producing an in-house magazine. He spent most of his time in the finance office, but as soon as the day's work was over, he would help in the kitchen or the laundry. He went on to take a degree in Business Management and was given work with pay during his breaks from college.

We also took visitors there at the end of their visits to the homes, to experience a safari. We would lunch at the Country Club and then they would take us to see the animals in the Safari Park, leaving us at the "The Ark" by the watering hole for the night. We would be collected from the lodge and returned to the Country Club the next morning. When I first started to take people to the lodge, just after the election troubles and we would be the only people there. The lodge could sleep one hundred guests, but as time went by the number of visitors increased for them. We continued to go as often as we could and the Country Club told us that they appreciated our support during the hard times and were happy to support us in return. Having made friends with the staff I was always warmly welcomed. One occasion stands out in my memory regarding a visit to the Ark. I walked into the viewing lounge where there were a few guests and a member of staff warmly welcomed me with a cup of tea, "Welcome Madam Ruth. Is there anything else I can do for you?" I looked out at the watering hole and there were very few animals there. "Please can you tell the elephants that I am here. I would like to see them." "Of course" he replied and as there were no more visitors waiting for tea, he left the room. He returned ten minutes later and said, "The elephants are on their way." We looked out of the window and a herd of about forty elephants came into view. It was such fun seeing the astonished expressions on the faces of the other guests, some of whom really thought he had called them.

Generally, people would greet me warmly as I was instantly recognisable, being the only white woman in the local area. I would offer lifts to anyone I passed on the road and take them into the local town. There was a particular stall in the market place of this town where I would buy my fruit and vegetables. The owner spoke good English and if she didn't have what I needed she would go to another stall for me. We became good friends and as a result, I was always able to trust the prices I was being charged.

Making friends with local people, being accepted and encouraged by them made life very normal for me. I was often invited into local homes and so, began to learn just how their lives worked. One of the most important things to learn was not to show shock at their living conditions just because they were different from mine and my expectations, as they were always proud of what they had and eager to share with me. Additionally, we also needed to show respect to the local authority, when working among the people in the community, consulting the chief when appropriate. Occasionally some people took the law into their own hands and did what they thought was right but always this had bad consequences. For example, one family was ostracised because of the help given to them by a well meaning visitor. Another example was misunderstanding people's greatest needs. Some families in the community were given items seen as their greatest need by the visitors, but these items were sold on, as their greatest need was food. A visit to the chief would have clarified the best way forward in each case.

God was showing me that it is so important in Christian experience, not to assume that what I see as the way forward for me is necessarily according to God's plan. I need to be in conversation with him daily to be sure that the way ahead is His and not mine.

5.2 Life is cheap

18 For you know that God paid a ransom to save you from the empty life you inherited from your ancestors. And it was not paid with mere gold or silver, which lose their value. 19 It was the precious blood of Christ, the sinless, spotless Lamb of God.
1 Peter 1:18-19 NLT

We have just been watching the news here in the UK (2023), where a young girl of 9 years old has been gunned down during a chase between drug dealers. She was nothing to them but everything to her family and friends. People die every day all over the world and the manner of their deaths is what matters to those who lose them.

In Kenya 'Life is cheap' seems to be the order of the day. Once, a car was hijacked very close to the boys' home and the owner was shot. It was only 7.00pm but it was already dark. Large stones had been placed across the road, so that the car had to stop, and the driver was wrenched from behind the wheel and shot. The car was driven away by the assailants. There was great consternation for my safety the following day and, when I was leaving the home at around 6.00pm, I was escorted by one of the older boys who then stayed with the staff in the girls home, and returned to the boys home the following morning.

I was always told not to travel after dark, but that is not so easy when darkness comes between 6 and 7 the whole year round. I was also told never to stop, if there was a body in the road, as this ploy was often used to make people stop. As soon as you stopped, there would be people hiding in the shadows who would come out and steal your car. I did drive around bodies, on some occasions, and this was hard to do as my instinct was to stop and help. I was told to vary my route home too, to make sure that I would not be caught out by familiarity and I was aware too, that often the "body" was someone who had passed out through drunkenness, which was very commonplace.

On one occasion I was returning from the Aberdare Country Club where the Home had a visiting team from the USA staying and I had been invited for a meal. It was at least 8.30pm and I realised that I should really be making my way home as it would take me at least 45 minutes driving in the dark. I said goodbye to everyone and began the drive home. I was faced with a choice of directions, either on the dirt roads or on the tarmac, each of which were potentially equally dangerous. I saw a pair of tail lights disappearing ahead on the dirt road and thought, well at least there is company. I followed but didn't see the car again. I went as fast as I could manage, as it was pitch dark and the road was rough. I eventually joined the tarmac road just outside our closest small town. Then, I was then stopped by a police checkpoint, where the policeman was very stern with me. "Where on earth have you been?" he asked. I explained I had been for a meal at the Country Club. He was very concerned for my safety and could not decide whether to leave his post and come with me or to let me continue. I explained it was only another 3 kilometres and I would go as fast as I could. He reluctantly let me go, making sure all my windows were closed and that I was locked in. I put my foot down and reached home safely, but decided it was not worth the risk in the future, so if I were invited to the Country Club again, I would book a room and stay the night. Learning wisdom!!

Rumours had circulated in our area about the fact that we had computers in our school, these had been donated by people in the USA. They were old, small, and of no real value as they had a free operating system, not related in any way to Microsoft or Apple, and no internet connection. We were able to use them with free word processing software with a view to helping our children have a chance to experience using a computer, as we knew that it would one day be part of their future. Unfortunately, it was assumed that they must be valuable. There was a gang operating in our area who were targeting many schools to steal paper, books and other supplies. We sounded like a juicy target for them. They came in the night. We had two guards who would patrol our grounds together. As they entered the school grounds to make sure all doors were locked, 20 young men wielding machetes came out of the dark. The guards ran and unlocked a classroom and tried to lock themselves in, but sadly they were too late, and they were viciously attacked and left for dead. Suddenly a pack of dogs came racing into the school grounds. These were our own guard dogs, who roamed freely at night. They attacked the intruders, who ran for their lives, leaving behind what they thought were two dead security men. Sadly, one of the guards had died but the other, in spite of his injuries, dragged himself out of the school and into the home, to find help. The police came, but obviously the gang were long gone. The effect on the home and the families of these brave men was enormous. They meant nothing to their attackers but everything to us. Amazingly, months later when he had recovered, the guard who had survived came back to the home to resume his duties because he loved caring for our children. He had a wonderful faith and trusted God even after such a terrible experience. When I was returning home he asked me for a bible in English and I was thrilled to give him a New Living Translation to help him read in English with confidence.

People in Kenya give thanks to the Lord all the time for surviving the night. It is no wonder when you see disease, poverty and sheer callousness in the behaviour of some people. It reminded me again how much we take for granted. There are those who suffer for a long time with illness but the immediacy of death is all around with so many factors that contribute to sudden death. Every day is precious to those who don't know where their next meal is coming from or are living with such danger hanging over them.

Being in danger is something we read about a lot in the Bible too. The Apostle Paul was constantly in danger.

In 2 Corinthians 11:23 -27 he writes :-

"I have been in prison more frequently, been flogged more severely, and been exposed to death again and again. 24 Five times I received from the Jews the forty lashes minus one. 25 Three times I was beaten with rods, once I was pelted with stones, three times I was shipwrecked, I spent a night and a day in the open sea, 26 I have been constantly on the move. I have been in danger from rivers, in danger from bandits, in danger from my fellow Jews, in danger from Gentiles; in danger in the city, in danger in the country, in danger at sea; and in danger from false believers. 27 I have laboured and toiled and have often gone without sleep; I have known hunger and thirst and have often gone without food; I have been cold and naked."

Why did Paul carry on with such awful things to face? His love for the Lord consumed him, hIs relationship with the Lord was so strong and the understanding of his mission gave him all the certainty he needed to carry on.

How does this look in my life? I realised that I too had to face the possibility of danger every time I went out, in a way that I had never been aware of at home. The Lord had not asked such suffering from me so far, but I had no idea what was ahead of me. I found myself talking to the Lord all the time even about trivial things. I began to look to scripture more and more for guidance and confirmation that I was doing the right thing. As I had learnt, I began to pray that I would know the Lord's presence with me every day, so that whatever happened I would be able to turn to him for the right response. I was reminded daily that I was here to fulfil the Lord's purposes and that I needed to do it in his way. There are very many wonderful verses to keep us strong in him.

Psalm 46:1,2 NLT

God is our refuge and strength, always ready to help in times of trouble.

2 So we will not fear when earthquakes come and the mountains crumble into the sea.

There is no danger which he does not know about.
Romans 8:35,37 NLT

35 Can anything ever separate us from Christ's love? Does it mean he no longer loves us if we have trouble or calamity, or are persecuted, or hungry, or destitute, or in danger, or threatened with death? 36 (As the Scriptures say, "For your sake we are killed every day; we are being slaughtered like sheep.") 37 No, despite all these things, overwhelming victory is ours through Christ, who loved us.

What wonderful words to help us face each uncertain day. I found that the more I read, the more I prayed, I found also that the more I sought to be right in the middle of God's plans for me, the more confident I felt and the less afraid of what could happen.

5.3 Behaviour

Learn to do right; seek justice. Defend the oppressed.
Take up the cause of the fatherless;
plead the case of the widow.
Isaiah 1:17 NIV

Every culture, whether in the east or the west, has hidden incidents of sexual misconduct which has become more apparent over recent years but, whilst in Kenya, it had not taken me long to learn that the culture there, at this time, contained a lot of hidden behaviours which were occasionally exposed by circumstances.

I had just returned after a visit home and my persecution started again. I had a male member of staff who had been a trusted friend, but now suddenly began to try and undermine my relationship with the children. I had always been very careful to ask permission if I did anything with the children. I would often go to the boys' home on a Saturday afternoon to play games with them as long as nothing else was planned. They had a formidable football team and played in a local league so on some occasions, I would take the ambulance, drive the team down to the village to play and then take them home again. Those not in the team would love to play card games, table tennis and board games while the footballers were enjoying practicing their skills. Sometimes they would go down to the river to swim. The community included the children from the homes in special events in the village and the local police college even came to teach the children how to march to their band. I joined in with them as much as I could and it was on one of these occasions when the trouble began. I felt as if my presence with the boys was resented. I would be chastised in front of the boys as if I had been doing things without permission, which was never true. I felt humiliated and angry. My instinct was to go home and lick my wounds but one of the older boys came alongside me and said, "I am so sorry for the way he is treating you Mum, but I think he is jealous because the boys love to see you and spend time with you." It gave me the strength to carry on and I decided that he was not going to drive me away. He then made his feelings known by always leaving the room when I entered it. The hostility continued and I was very concerned about it as I found that some of the older children were taken away from my area of responsibility. I later discovered, if I was seen talking to them, they would be punished after I had gone home.

I then found that a staff member had been transferred to the home where I had helped with the Early Years class and everything I had made for the nursery class was destroyed and burned. It was as if they wanted to wipe away everything I had done for them. It is hard to describe how this hatred made me feel. I was angry, frustrated and I felt helpless, so I decided that it was best for me to be very careful with anything I was involved in, in order to minimise the adverse effect on the children.

We also had a sad case of abuse to deal with, in the home where I was living, where the police were called and the man arrested. A counsellor was called in to help the children deal with their experience and to understand what to do if they experienced unacceptable behaviour from an adult. This was difficult, for some of the children, as it was often their nearest trusted relative who had caused them pain in the past.

Hidden behaviours were occasionally exposed by circumstances. I knew of one child at the age of eight who was sexually assaulted by her uncle, who had been given the responsibility to care for her while her father went to seek work, and this came to light when the child contracted syphilis.

Another occasion was when I had to take my house girl to the hospital in the middle of the night because she felt so ill. While we were waiting for her to receive treatment, a family arrived with a seven year old girl who had just been raped by a neighbour.

More abuse was uncovered, and at last the real reason for all the hostility became known to me. There was a real fear that if I got too close to the children I would find out about abusive activities among our children, and I did. Many of the children in our care had been rescued from abusive situations, so I had to learn how to deal with the emotional trauma that our children were experiencing, and trying to deal with. I had never had such experiences before and felt very much out of my depth. More than ever before, I needed the guidance from the Lord. I had to listen to many extremely traumatic stories of bullying and abuse, and somehow to reassure these children that we understood and would take action as necessary. They begged me not to tell anyone about what had been happening to them as it made them feel ashamed. I told them I could not deal with this on my own, so they gave me a few trusted names, and I passed on what I knew to them. I sought justice for these children and passed on my information to the Charity who took the necessary steps to legally deal with the abuser and we brought in a Christian counsellor who was able to spend time with all the children who needed to talk these things through. How could I really help these children in a way that would bring peace to them and hope for the future? I searched the internet for ways of using Scripture to deal with this sin and build up the lives of these young people again. I called my own brother who was a counsellor and we discussed the approach that I needed to take. It was so helpful to talk with someone who had real insight into trauma. I then began to put together God's view of sin, responsibility and reconciliation, as shown in Scripture and we found that this was really helpful to some of the older children who could discuss their own problems which had arisen as a consequence of abuse. But I also had to deal with my own emotions, I was often so deeply upset that I would listen to the children and then go home and cry. I was experiencing a side of life that I knew was there, but which had never impacted on me before. The Counsellor was also a help to me too, as I talked about the situation with her. After listening, she told me that in her opinion the Lord had brought me to Kenya for such a time as this, because the children involved, finally had someone to talk to who would listen and not judge them.

5.4 Forgiveness

37 "Do not judge, and you will not be judged.
Do not condemn, and you will not be condemned.
Forgive, and you will be forgiven.
Luke 6:37 NIV

There was more fallout from this very challenging time, as people and their behaviour were exposed, they had to bear the consequences. It was decided that it was not safe for me to be driving about, because of the people who now had to face those consequences, could bear a grudge. It was feared that I would be forced off the road if I was seen in my car. I realised too, that someone was going around the villages and nearby towns telling lies about me to cover their own behaviour, and as a result there were many people who no longer trusted me or wanted anything to do with me. I was ostracised by many people in the community. I was devastated. I was trying to do the right thing and was suffering the backlash. All I wanted to do was go out into the villages and towns to declare my innocence and expose those who were really to blame for the situation. I had to decide that my only response would be to pray and read my bible even though I was in great distress, as all this seemed to be so unfair. Suddenly the Lord showed me a precious promise.

Romans 8:33-34

33 Who will bring any charge against those whom God has chosen? It is God who justifies. 34 Who then is the one who condemns? No one. Christ Jesus who died—more than that, who was raised to life—is at the right hand of God and is also inter ceding for us.

So, here it is, the next big lesson of care from my Heavenly Father. I do not need to go and justify myself to these people, because it is God who justifies. These words hit me because it was the same word "justify". I only needed to be justified to God and Jesus had done that for me when he died on the cross and rose again. I felt that the Lord was telling me to trust him to sort this out and what I needed to do was to get on with the work I had been given to do.

I had previously had the backing of a pastor, from the local town near the boys home, for my work with the boys bible study group, but now he was disappointed to hear all the rumours about me. He came to the home to speak with our own pastor, who reassured him that all the rumours were false. Unknown to me, it was decided to put me to the test. The nearest small town had seven churches who all got together to hold a youth rally and I was invited to be part of the team. They gave me a small group to work with. We had the main teaching session and then went into our groups for discussions. I had one of the pastors in with me and we completed the tasks given. At the end of the day I was invited to have tea with the seven pastors and we discussed how the day had gone. I was thanked for my part in the day and they told me that if they ever did this again they would like me to be one of the speakers. I have no idea what they had heard and I have no idea what they were looking for in me, but God had made it clear that I could be trusted. It must have taken about two years to fully restore me, in the eyes of the community, but the Lord kept to his word "I am the one who justifies" I am sure that **not** listening to the gossip about me had helped me to remain faithful to the work God had given me to do, and not worry about people who may be against me.

I still had my own personal challenges to deal with that were there as a result of this situation. For a while, some of the boys would not speak to me, as I had caused so much disruption to their lives, but eventually they softened, in their attitude towards me, and our friendship continued. I found that I was very angry at one person in particular. His behaviour had shocked me and I hated him for all the distress he had caused to many, including me, so I wanted to see him punished and I wanted the punishment to hurt. I was very upset when reading my bible to see that God was telling me to 'love my enemies.' I don't think I had ever considered anyone in particular to be my enemy until now. I kept telling the Lord, in my distress, that it was impossible to love anyone like this. How could I possibly show love to someone whose behaviour was so hateful? I spent many hours trying to make sense of this particular instruction from the Lord. It came to a head when one day I was starting a journey to Nairobi, and my car was full of students and equipment to deliver. I was actually going through the 'love your enemy' passage in my head and there he was at the side of the road. It was as if the Lord was saying, "Yes, this one" and I knew that I had somehow got to get to the bottom of this problem and put God's instructions into place.

After the journey I sent a message to my daughter to ask her for her understanding of this passage. She wrote back saying, " Anyone who does not love the Lord is going to have to face the wrath of God, and you would not want that for anyone, even your worst enemy. Pray that he comes to repentance. That is the most loving thing you can do for anyone." "Yes", I thought, "that I can do." So from that day I prayed for his repentance, not his destruction. It also led me to thinking about forgiveness, and of course, the Lord pointed out, through his word, that we need to forgive to bring about the healing of our own hearts. If we live with unforgiveness in our hearts we will be full of bitterness. They still have to face God themselves for their forgiveness before him but we need to forgive them ourselves because, let's face it, we too have been forgiven for everything we have done. Saying that you forgive someone does not mean that what they did was OK. It was not OK, and they still have to face the consequences of their sin. We have to remember that we have been forgiven by God for every sin that we have ever, or may ever, commit. We have no right to withhold forgiveness from someone else.

This was a very precious lesson to learn and has taught me never to hate anyone for what they have done but to pray for their restoration and reconciliation to God himself.

5.5 Responding to the unexpected

"Who has known the mind of the Lord?
Or who has been his counsellor?"
35 "Who has ever given to God,
that God should repay them?"
Romans 11:34,35 NIV

I began to realise that when asking God to help me or keep me safe, this was rather unspecific. Life here was so unpredictable that I never knew what I would be asked to do at any given time. My morning prayer was always to ask God to help me be aware that he was with me so that whatever I was facing he would guide me through and, no matter what the day may bring I knew I was in good hands

> Romans 15:13 says *"May the God of hope fill you with all joy and peace as you trust in him, so that you may overflow with hope by the power of the Holy Spirit."*

I was travelling into our local town one morning. The drive was beautiful, and I always enjoyed the half hour journey, as it took us down into a valley with a steep climb up to the town. As I descended into the valley, I joined a long line of cars waiting to proceed. There had obviously been some kind of incident ahead but I could not see what it was. I waited until a man, who had been looking at each of the vehicles in the queue, reached mine. I don't know why he chose me in particular, but my car was a four by four and I wasn't carrying passengers or goods. He told me there had been an accident between a motorbike and a lorry on the bridge below. One passenger on the motorbike had been thrown into the river and swept away, but there was another man, with a broken leg who needed to go to hospital, so he asked, 'could I take him?' I was happy to do that but told him that I would want someone to come with me to help when we reached the hospital. He readily agreed and brought another man to accompany me. I pulled out of the line of traffic and went to the bridge. In the distance we could see a crowd of people searching the river for the missing man, but it was decided that I should go ahead to the hospital with the injured man. They lifted him into the back where he lay along the seat. He profusely thanked me and asked for my phone number, which I refused to give, because I knew it would end with requests for money, so I told him that my contribution to his situation was the journey to the hospital. As we began to climb the hill there was a shout from the valley, saying they had found the other man, so we pulled over to the side of the road and waited. They carried him to the car and placed him in the far back. His leg was clearly broken too, with bone showing, and he was bleeding. As soon as he was in, we went as fast as we could to the hospital. When we arrived, my helper leapt out and went to organise the trolleys/stretchers to take the men into the emergency department. I said goodbye and continued with my own tasks for the day, followed by washing out the blood from the far back of the car.

News of the men filtered through to me, so I knew they had both survived and were well. Even though I had been careful not to give my number, soon I had a text message on my phone from the young man, telling me how much his medical bill was going to be. I wrote back and wished him well but reiterated that I had already played my part.

Some weeks later I was on my way to Nanyuki, a town at the equator, and I was stopped at a police check point as usual. The policeman walked round my car and told me that one of my tail lights was not working. He had spotted this as I stopped. He told me he was going to charge me quite a lot of money for this infringement, a few thousand shillings. The hardest thing when this happens is not to argue as 85-90% of vehicles on the road either had faulty lights or no working lights at all. I said I would get it fixed straight away, but he became very officious and told me that he was arresting me. He ordered another policeman to get into my car and to take me to the police station. According to their own handbook, which I carried with me, at no time is a police officer allowed to get into a private car. I decided that it would not be helpful to point this out to him, at this moment, so we went to the police station, where I left the young people who were with me in the car asking them to pray for me. I didn't want to get put into the cells and leave the young people stranded. Inside the policemen were very kind but they got out the relevant paperwork and began to question me. They were very surprised that I had been arrested and asked if I had been rude to the officer, so I said that I didn't think I had. We began to talk about the reason for my presence in Kenya and they were very interested to hear about the work of the Charity. One of them told me he had a friend who had a lot of mattresses and maybe he could give them to the Charity. I had learned to be very wary of this kind of offer, as I had no idea where these mattresses were from. I explained that this was not my department but I would pass on the message. By the time we had finished the conversation they decided that I did not have to pay the fine of 5,000 shillings but I should go and get the bulb fixed straight away. "Don't get the 50 shilling bulb as it will not last so get the 80 shilling one" was the parting advice. I went straight to the garage where I always took my car to be serviced and he did the job for me straight away.

You may wonder at the relevance of these two stories together. I had been learning over the months of being in Kenya to look to the Lord carefully when it came to money, as the poverty, and other great needs around, can lead you into randomly giving money that may then be misspent or not actually be filling the need in question. One thing the Lord was also showing me was how to be generous especially after he had blessed me. I felt that having been let off the fine I was now in a position to bless someone else, should the opportunity arise. That opportunity came a few days later.

I was on another journey to town and as I climbed out of the valley, there was a man on crutches trying to climb the very steep hill. This time I was driving the pickup but I stopped to offer him a lift. To my astonishment it was the same young man, from the original accident, making his way into town to get an x ray for his leg. He had walked all the way from our small town to this point and it must have taken him hours. He climbed into the back of the pickup and we drove into town. Once there I ascertained the cost of the x ray and gave him the 5,000 shillings so that he could have the x ray and pay for transport back home. We became good friends and it was lovely to see him make progress until he was walking normally again.

Acts 20;35 Paul says,

> **35** *"In everything I did, I showed you that by this kind of hard work we must help the weak, remembering the words the Lord Jesus himself said: 'It is more blessed to give than to receive.'"*

5.6 Sin

23 The Lord directs the steps of the godly.
He delights in every detail of their lives.
24 Though they stumble, they will never fall,
for the Lord holds them by the hand.
Psalm 37:23-24 NLT

People do not like the word sin as it conjures up a picture of things that are very bad. We categorise sin to make it easier for ourselves and we have big sins, and little sins, but God does not regard sin by degree. For him sin is sin, no matter whether it is big or small in our eyes. The dictionary says it is 'the transgression of divine law'. We need to come to him in repentance when we have sinned knowing that forgiveness is there.

The longer I stayed in Kenya the more I became aware of the difference in our cultures, of the way society operated, and so many things that were not available but would have been commonplace at home. An example of this was when a colleague had a problem with an electrical item which she had bought from a store in town. When we took it back to the shop with the receipt, the man looked at us in astonishment, amazed we told him we were returning the item because it didn't work. We asked for a replacement and he just laughed. "Why would I do that?" he asked. We pointed out that he had a responsibility to sell things that were in good working order. We went round and round in circles and we were obviously not going to get a replacement until suddenly he said "Ok, I will change it for you." We were very surprised, but happy with the outcome until as we were leaving the shop, we saw him put our one back on the shelf to sell to some other poor unaware shopper and, of course when we got home the new one didn't work either. From that time on we only bought from a store where they unpacked the item you were buying, and plugged it in to make sure it was working. Or if the item were large, they would deliver it with a staff member who would set up the item in your house and check it there. I could understand their hesitation to change items, because people could have broken it themselves after buying it, but the human heart is deeply corrupt, even in small things, and that makes me very sad. The corruption around in all walks of life was so rife that I had to become very cautious as some people would see a white person as fair game, and it was easy to spend so much more than things were worth. I could understand this attitude too, as, during our British occupation of Kenya, we were far from just in our dealings with people. If in doubt I would take a trusted friend with me and in this way I built up friendships with local people who then treated me with respect. I would take visitors to the equator, where there were gift shops for tourists, but beforehand I gave our visitors a talk about how to haggle and what was generally fair, visitors would be overcharged if the shop owners could get away with it.. After being there for so many years, my friendship with these traders was built on mutual respect and, before I came home, they were kind enough to give me a gift for supporting them.

That was just one aspect, fairness and honesty in trading, where sin was easy and relatively "small" in our thinking and manageable with care but I also became very aware of people who had one face for you when you were around, and another behind your back, when their behaviour was hidden from sight. Does that sound familiar? It is the same the world over. It is the way most people behave when they are guilty of something that they wish to hide from others. When we interviewed for new staff, we had a panel of people to ask the searching questions, to see if we could be sure of the character of the person we would employ. We always prayed before the interviews for the discernment and wisdom we needed to make the right decisions. Often, we found that one candidate stood out from the rest and, over the years, we have employed some very godly and dedicated people and we praised God for that. Once in a while, though, we did not get it right and found ourselves having to remove members of staff because of hidden behaviour that only came to light later. When I was around, the children were all treated well because they knew my views on discipline, but I discovered that, for one member of staff, beating the children was her solution for everything. We had a strict regime of ways to discipline the children and there was no place for random beatings. We had suspicions about another member of staff's honesty whilst looking at the financial transactions, they did not make sense. We sent someone in to take a look in greater detail and he uncovered a mare's nest of corruption. The more we looked the more we found, and not just financial theft but stealing in other ways too. His thieving was to the detriment of the home's children but to the benefit of his own family. Sadly, we had to remove him, but he would not admit that he had been wrong, his response was to criticise everything I was doing to deflect guilt from himself.

Lying was a common way of dealing with issues, and this was a minefield for me to walk through, but, this is also so common to us all. We even have the phrase "white lies" as if there are lies that don't qualify as real lies. I had to deal with many issues where I had to work through the situation, to uncover the lies, before I could get to the truth but the Lord always helped me in doing this. Knowing how the human heart operates and, having the Holy Spirit to help and guide my way through, was so essential to everything I was doing. I did not expect to be spending my time like this in my sixties and I often felt rather overwhelmed, but the Lord was very gracious to me and held my hand at all times. Why did I have to go through all this? Looking back, the children needed someone who would listen to them, without jumping to conclusions and judgements, and eventually, they knew they could trust me.

Judging others is rife among all of us. Every time we gossip, we are passing judgement on our friends and acquaintances. The culture in Kenya was one where judgements were very quickly made and children, in particular were considered complicit when the fault was actually with the adult. Making people feel guilty seemed often to be the object of the exercise and pointing the finger at others was the solution. We often judge by appearances without knowing the background or circumstances of the person we are condemning.

Do you remember the story in John 8:1-11? A woman is brought before Jesus who had been caught in the act of adultery. The men who brought her wanted to trap Jesus into saying something that they could use against him, so they asked him if they should stone her. After constant questioning Jesus said *"Let any one of you who is without sin be the first to throw a stone at her."* One by one the men left the scene and it even tells us that it was the older men who left first. Eventually Jesus looks up, and he has been left alone with the woman. *He says, "Woman, where are they? Has no one condemned you?"* **11** *"No one, sir," she said. "Then neither do I condemn you," Jesus declared. "Go now and leave your life of sin."*

It was so easy to point the finger until Jesus pointed to the guilt in all of us. It wasn't just that she had been forgiven, but also she was told, along with that forgiveness, she needed to leave behind her former life of sin.

That is what we all need to learn. Jesus came to take the punishment for our sin, and he did that on the cross. He gives us new life in him, and our responsibility is to live the life that we have been given, to the glory of God. That means being aware of our sin, coming to the Lord in repentance every day, knowing that this sin has already been forgiven but that we need to learn from the Holy Spirit how to go on to live each day without that sin. We are human beings and we will fall again and again but the amazing thing is that we do not have to live with the guilt of the past, we just need to grow in our love and life for Jesus.

5.7 Blessings

He gives strength to the weary
and increases the power of the weak.
Isaiah 40:29 NIV

Another Christmas had come and, by now, we had sent as many children to their families as we could, to build up the relationships that would be needed when the children finally left our care. Some of the homes were able to send all their children to wider families but, where I was living, we still had about fifteen children with nowhere to go. We wanted to make this time special for them and I produced some activity books to share with them. They had a lovely time, in our own little church in the morning, celebrating the birth of Jesus, and then we provided a lovely Christmas meal. All the children had been taken out to choose special clothes for Christmas a few days prior to the event, and this was always considered a very special day when visiting the shops in town. The afternoon was spent playing games and generally enjoying the time together. In the evening, they watched a film. Frozen was a firm favourite!

Unfortunately, this particular year, a week before Christmas I had become ill. I had no idea what was wrong, I just felt feverish and sick, and I was exhausted. I assumed I had been overdoing things. Eventually I took to my bed with some painkillers, and hoped some rest would make the difference.

On Christmas morning I got up determined to get across the field to church, but I could only get half way, before needing to sit down, so I made my way back to my bungalow. Fortunately someone had seen my pathetic attempt and came to see how I was. One look at me and they decided I probably had malaria and typhoid together, which is not uncommon. The pastor took me to the hospital in our ambulance, no sirens! It was just the only vehicle that was available!

There was no GP service where I was so, if you needed a doctor you had to go to the hospital. I was taken to the doctor and, after examination, I was sent to the blood test department. Here it was normal to have the test done, wait for the results and go back to the doctor straight away. I did this and on checking the results he said, "You will be pleased to know that it is not malaria or typhoid but a severe bacterial infection. He prescribed two kinds of antibiotic and sent me to the pharmacy. At this point, I had not even given payment a thought, my mind had been too tired to think about it. While I was waiting for the medication and the bill, my phone beeped with an incoming message. To my astonishment it was a dear friend from my home church who had visited me with his wife on several occasions. He told me "I am sitting here in church, on Christmas morning and I have no idea why I am doing this, but I am sending you 5,000 shillings, so here it is. The money arrived immediately through the mpesa system. Then my name was called to collect my medication and pay the bill which was 4,900 shillings, the spare 100 shillings went towards the cost of the fuel for the ambulance. My heart was filled with thankfulness for the attention to detail that had come from the Lord that day. It was such a joy to share this with my friends from home so that they could see how the Lord had used them to bless me that day.

Blessings are strange things as, so often, they are only seen as financial, particularly in this culture. I had gone through another period of learning how I should respond to people who offered me help, in one way or another. I have quite an independent spirit and, it seemed wrong to accept things if I felt I could manage for myself. Then one day when I was reading my bible, I came across this verse in Galatians 6:9

"So let's not get tired of doing what is good. At just the right time we will reap a harvest of blessing if we don't give up."

It suddenly occurred to me, by refusing to be blessed by people who wanted to help I was denying them the possibility of a harvest of blessings!! So I was not to be selfish, and see myself as the one who was blessing people I met, but, that I should also accept that I was the one that others wanted to help.

I had not yet fully understood that position when I had call from a close friend, asking me to go home to be at her upcoming wedding. I really wanted to be there but did not have enough money, at that point, for the flight. One of the problems involved was that it was going to be at a very expensive time of year for travel, and my funds were limited. I didn't want to tell her this so I just said that I would try my best, and began to think about ways to save enough money. Unknown to me, she and her future husband saw through my attempt to hide my situation and they went ahead and bought my ticket for me. So, the Lord was going to make this very clear to me without my own input. I discovered this kindness, of buying my ticket, during the visit of another friend, but to add to this blessing for me, another family, from my church, had upgraded the ticket to first class. Feeling very overwhelmed by this generosity I had a wonderful trip home.

I was able to host people sometimes who wanted to come and work alongside me, and these were very special times as it gave me a chance to share the load. One young lady came for two years and we each had our own area of work. Our Charity were very concerned to make sure that we were emotionally strong, and gave us time to take a break in many different ways. We went to a conference for missionaries, from many organisations, in Nairobi with the title "Serving from a place of Rest". This was very encouraging.

We took a trip to Zambia for one month because there were more elections taking place in Kenya and it was deemed to be unsafe for us to stay there. The Charity had work in Zambia and, once again I was able to do some staff training. It was a wonderful trip including walking with lions, a visit to Victoria Falls and a trip along the Zambezi where we experienced the most glorious sunset.

I also had the privilege of travelling to the States, to help with a fund raising project, where I met some wonderful, generous people and also reacquainted myself with many of the visitors who had come to Kenya in teams. My return flight also had been quite an adventure. I was at the airport in time, but my flight was severely delayed by weather conditions, so as we sat waiting to take off I knew then that my connecting flight in New York would be gone by the time I got there. When we arrived in New York I was met by someone with a notice with my name on it, the airline had rearranged my flight. After running through the airport, I was the last person to get on the plane, but we then sat on the tarmac for more than an hour, by which time, I knew my flight to Kenya, from London, would be gone. When we landed in London, I approached the very busy desk and asked for a hotel overnight and a flight the next day. They were only too pleased to do that for me, rather than seeking an alternative route. Finally I landed in Nairobi the following day and amazingly, despite everything that had happened, my luggage was waiting for me.

So many blessings.

- The Lord being with me as I faced persecution.

- Teaching me how to forgive and therefore healing my own heart.

- Showing me how many blessings were coming my way.

- Making me so aware of his loving care.

6. Learning it is all about Him, not about me

6.1 Relationships

Lord, you are my God; I will exalt you and praise
your name, for in perfect faithfulness you have
done wonderful things, things planned long ago.
Isaiah 25:1 NIV

I had been reading Ezekiel 16. It is a chapter where God likens his relationship with his nation Israel to the life of a young woman. He was there at the beginning of life, he cared for and nurtured her, he clothed her and surrounded her with the best of everything. In return she prostituted herself to anyone who came along, not even charging them but giving herself to anyone who wanted her. She used all the blessings she had been given to make idols and to please others. She even sacrificed her own children to worthless gods.

Such a sad, startling story, but very clear in its meaning, showing the relationship of God with his people Israel. It made me think about our lives and how we look for happiness and value, in so many different ways but fail to find it. We ignore what God is offering, mistakenly thinking it comes with strings we don't want.

We seek satisfaction in relationships and these do not always turn out the way we would like. Polygamy is allowed in Kenya, and I saw the results in the lives of many of the women I met. To be a second or third wife, for some, was better than not being married at all. We had a young girl, Miriam, turn up at the Charity who was really just a child, about 12 years old, but she was heavily pregnant and had nowhere to go. A staff member took her in and, after she gave birth, she and her baby stayed with them. They employed her as their house-girl and helped with the baby. This was a great blessing to her, and to them, as their own children were very young. All was well until at the age of about 15 when she met a young man who wanted to take her as his second wife. He had had an argument with his first wife, and she and their child had gone back to her mother. Miriam was under age, but they could not stop her from constantly running away, back to him. Eventually he took her officially as his second wife but she had left her own child behind as he did not want another child that was not his. Of course, the day came when the first wife returned and naturally difficult problems grew within that household, but there was no going back. Human solutions fall so far short of what God intended for us, when he created us.

Going back to the story in Ezekiel. God had developed the nation of Israel with a clear purpose, He wanted her to be a beacon to the surrounding nations, in order that they could see that God was the only true and real God. It was only in their relationship with him that they would find the love, the kindness and the value that they wanted. He wants us to put him first, to follow the way that he leads, to find everything we need in him and, to be a beacon of light to all those around us who are still living in darkness. Too often we think other things will be more satisfying than putting God first.

We also wanted to be a beacon of light to those around us, as well as caring for the children. It was our desire that these children would have a real relationship with the living God. On leaving the homes they would need to know also that God cares for them and we wanted them to learn to trust him. Without God what would they have as a future? We wanted them to learn to put God first in everything.

The small communities around us were also part of the lives of the homes and we relied on local people to come and work with us. We used local labour as much as we could. If a team came from abroad we did not use only them to do the maintenance work that was needed, even though that was free of cost for us. A visiting team would pay for the supplies and then provide the labour, but we also made sure that we employed local labour to do things the way they would be done in the locality. This employment was very important to these people. It also helped us to build good relationships with those around us. I had a house-girl, not because I couldn't run my own house but because she needed employment. I had two different girls during my time there, the first one was a lovely girl who took great care of me, but her real desire was to become a nurse. When the opportunity arose for her to follow her ambition, I then employed her sister. We tried some community projects too, giving local people chickens to begin to provide a little income for the family, by selling the eggs and rearing chickens to be eaten. Some families were given a goat too, so they could use the milk. They would also breed from the goat to provide meat for sale, as well as for the family. A cow would be given to provide milk and also to breed from. Their firstborn goat or cow was then given back, to be passed on to another family.

One of our real success stories was a woman who started with chickens and then began breeding goats. She was then able to buy herself a cow to begin more breeding. Eventually, she hired a piece of land to grow crops and keep her animals. She ended up with a small shop in the village to sell her produce. This showed what could be achieved.

6.2 How will I know?

So do not fear, for I am with you;
do not be dismayed, for I am your God.
I will strengthen you and help you;
I will uphold you with my righteous right hand.
Isaiah 41:10 NIV

How would I know when it would be time for me to go home?
I was by now 68 years old and wondered if the Lord still had
work for me to finish, or even to start. The school was well
established and growing each year. The head teacher was a
wonderfully godly and humble man and God was using him to
build up the work for the glory of God. The independence
programme was running well and my role now was visiting the
different homes to deal with staff issues where necessary and
generally encourage the work. In fact, much of my time was
spent driving between all our homes, approximately 1,000 miles
for the round trip.

God speaks in many different ways, and I decided to pray
about my situation. Because of my increasing age I did not
want to end up as a burden to anyone. I prayed that the Lord
would help me to make the right decision at the right time. I
was feeling homesick for my family as my grandchildren were
growing up fast. I prayed that God would give me the strength
to fulfil his purposes in his timing. I was due to travel to
America, via the UK, to attend the marriage of my co-worker
from the States, but I then began to feel unwell. I was used to
having occasional flare-ups of a condition called Sarcoidosis,
which I had had since my mid-twenties. However, by now they
were infrequent and very mild. Usually a few days' rest, and I
was ok. I felt pain all over my body, but especially in my joints,

so I rested, but this time there was no improvement, in fact it was getting considerably worse. In Kenya I could get strong painkillers over the counter so I consulted my medical friends and had one recommended to me. I bought enough for my journey plus a few days' worth extra and intended to visit my own doctor once I was home. This could not have happened at a worse time. I was determined to go, if I could make it at all, and so I booked my flight home, so that I could travel onwards from there to meet the correct dates for the wedding. I had been asked to get some small bags of coffee, that could be given to the guests at the wedding. When I reached the guest house in Nairobi, the manager helped me by ordering the coffee to be delivered to the guest house for me. There were 250 small bags. At the airport they decided to search my luggage and looked in amazement at the bags of coffee. I explained about the wedding and they laughed at this strange idea. Most Kenyans drink tea rather than coffee, even though they grow both.

The journey was long and I was still in a lot of pain. Having arrived home I went to visit my doctor who kindly prescribed the medication. She told me to go and enjoy the wedding and, she would follow it up when I returned. Unfortunately, the painkillers prescribed were not strong enough to deal with the level of pain I was experiencing. I prayed for the strength I needed to survive this trip. The thought of going through customs with 250 bags of coffee was an adventure in itself. I know coffee is often used to cover the smell of drugs and I didn't want to get arrested!!

I flew to the States but found that I could barely walk when it was time to leave the plane. I managed to make my way slowly but then could not lift my luggage from the carousel. Fortunately, there were some very kind people who stepped forward and helped me. I had declared the volume of coffee in my luggage, and no one seemed interested, so I passed through customs with no problem. I was met by a family member of my colleague and we began the drive home. She was very kind to me and we reached our destination in good time. It was lovely to meet the family and we had a wonderful time together. They even added the unexpected help of getting me some stronger medication which made life a great deal easier for me.

It was a delightful time, being with them all again, and the day of the wedding arrived. We had the ceremony, followed by the reception, in a marquee in the garden. I was placed at a table where I met a lovely lady, about eighty years old, and we had an interesting conversation. As we talked, she suddenly said to me, "Are you the lady who lives on the mountain in Kenya?" I was a bit surprised and said "Probably." It transpired that she had heard of me through the family and had been praying for me. Then in great surprise to both of us she said quite clearly, "Your time in Kenya has come to an end." She looked as shocked as I felt. She went on to say, "I have never done that before but I know it's true. You must not rush to finish, but you need to spend the next two years preparing to leave, so that everything is handed over in an orderly manner." Well for me it was the answer to my prayer but I was surprised because it was so direct and clear. She had no idea I had just two years left on my Visa and the prospect of being able to renew it successfully was becoming more remote. This seemed a fitting conclusion to my adventure, it having started with someone telling me God wanted me in Kenya, and now someone telling me God wanted me to go home.

On my return to England, I decided not to return to my own doctor but to go to a clinic in London that specialised in tropical diseases, just in case my condition was more complicated. I only had a few days left before I was due to fly back to Kenya and, at this moment I felt unable to contemplate a return. On the Thursday I met a young doctor who had been born and grew up in Kenya and she diagnosed me with

Polymyalgia, and said that what I needed was a neurologist. She had access to two so she would get me an appointment and call me. I went home and the call came. She had been unable to get me the appointment and asked if I had any way of finding a neurologist myself. By now I was praying that the Lord would really step in here, as I was willing to return to Kenya but, how on earth could I make it in this condition? On the Friday, two of my close friends bumped into each other at the supermarket and happened to discuss my dilemma. One was a retired senior nurse with a retired doctor husband, and medical contacts, and she immediately said that she could get me the necessary appointment, but it would involve a journey to Cambridge, where she and her husband would be happy to drive me. She called me later in the day to say the doctor had agreed to see me, but he would be at a private clinic, only three miles away from my own home, on the Saturday morning.

It is very exciting to be in God's hands and watch all the pieces of the jigsaw coming together. We went to the clinic on the Saturday and met the consultant, who asked me lots of questions about my time in Kenya. At the end of the consultation he told me that he would not be charging me anything for this appointment. I felt as if I was in a bit of a whirlwind. He agreed with the Polymyalgia diagnosis and gave me a steroid injection, but I was not to use any painkillers for the next two days. Then I was to phone him at a precise time to tell him how I was feeling. I went home to rest and found an email prescription for more steroids in my inbox. The pain was terrible and I did nothing for the next two days. I was due to fly to Kenya on the Tuesday and on Monday morning I could barely walk. When the time arrived for the phone call, it was as if someone had flipped a switch and, suddenly I could walk, as the pain had begun to reduce. Armed with my new medication, I was on the plane the next day with no problem at all.

I arrived back in Nairobi and discovered that a branch of the same London clinic had just opened there, so I registered myself. The internet connection with the London clinic meant that all my records were available online and it made life much easier for me as I was able to have regular checkups until I was cleared. I even met the young lady doctor from London again, who had decided to come home to Kenya. They were all such delightful and very helpful people.

It was such a wonderful miracle filled adventure and it gave me such confidence to follow through the instructions I had been given to prepare for going home.

I also wondered why I had been spared the cost of everything, because I could have found the money, and recalled the incident with the man on crutches and his x ray. When I returned to the home it was as if the Lord was saying to me, "Let me show you the next part of the story." One of our staff members was on chemotherapy and had reached the end of her resources before having the last course. I knew immediately that it would cost the same amount as my treatment would have cost and sure enough it was so. It meant I was able to fund her treatment and she was able to continue to improve in health. Frequently I found that God would bless me so that I could pass that blessing on. When she told me she didn't know how to say thank you enough, I was able to encourage her to do the same through her life, if God blesses you then pass the blessing on.

6.3 Caring

No power in the sky above or in the earth below—
indeed, nothing in all creation will ever be able to
separate us from the love of God that is
revealed in Christ Jesus our Lord.
Romans 8:39 NLT

The young people who now had left the home and were settling down to fend for themselves, still considered me to be their "Mum", which meant phone calls any time of the day or night so I had to set my phone to "Do not disturb" after 10pm. I even had a call one night from a boy who had been stabbed. He was living two hours journey away so all I could do was to let the relevant staff members know and pray that he would be safe. We visited him a couple of days later and found that he had been taken to hospital by a passer-by. The hospital team discovered that the knife had missed all his vital organs, so he survived.

Another night, I had a frantic call from Jacob, who had become the target for men who wanted to recruit him for scamming people into being blackmailed. He had answered a call from another one of our boys, Amos who had been scammed and then arrested, and by men who appeared to be policemen. The two boys had managed to get away from them, but were now being pursued. Amos had disappeared from the house leaving his phone behind and now Jacob could see the men knocking on doors in his street. He called me because he needed money for transport but I had none to give on that day. He had recently bought a motorbike and managed to borrow enough money from someone to refuel it. He was so afraid of being caught that he took a very remote route and ended up at my door at 4.00am. We then had to decide how to find Amos. Later in the morning we began calling anyone who may know where he was, but we couldn't find a trace of him. We were so worried and called on everyone we knew and asked them to pray for him. A couple of days later Amos turned up on my doorstep. He had seen the men approaching the house and was so scared he ran off without even thinking about his phone. He went to the home of a classmate from college and his friend's father took him in and hid him. They had suffered from a similar incident themselves and were very willing to help. Amos could not stay long because it would put this family in danger as well. As soon as he could, he made his way to my house. We then had to decide what to do next, as they were too afraid to return to their normal lives. Suddenly the news broke of a major incident in Nairobi and the whole of Kenya was in shock. Terrorists had taken over an upmarket shopping mall. This mall was where the more wealthy or important people would shop. They had hostages and were threatening to kill anyone who could not quote from the Koran. The hostages were trying to help each other. This was retribution for Kenyan military trying to help fight terrorism in Somalia. 71 people died, including the terrorists, 200 were wounded and it lasted 4 days.

We realised, with such an awful situation to deal with, this would mean no one would be interested in Jacob and Amos anymore so they found a new place to live and returned to normality.

Scams were becoming more frequent, and our students now had mobile phones, and access to the Internet but thankfully no one had any money to spare. We needed to educate them to spot and ignore the scams, so this was added to our training sessions.

I spent all my time now visiting and caring for our students. I travelled all over the country and I never tired of the amazing views throughout Kenya. The Rift Valley, so deep and wide, and the tea plantations in Kericho were spectacular, with tea growing as far as the eye could see. I went to different colleges, meeting tutors, making sure that our young people were living in suitable conditions and working hard at their courses. We had given them a contract to sign, when they went to college, to help them understand the seriousness of what they were doing and the fact that someone had provided for them to take this step in their lives. Some sponsors came and met the children for themselves to encourage them in their endeavours, and this was often life changing for both the student and the sponsor. I would drive them to all the relevant places. Not all students kept to their contract and there were times when I had to decide on the disciplinary measures to get them back on track. This was never easy but it was necessary in order to help them to understand responsibility. Not all students completed their courses and found themselves back seeking casual work. However we did have some great successes. The face to face contact with our students was hugely important to them and it was always then a joy to be there for their graduations when we could.

How was I going to leave these young people? I had the mother hen instinct and wanted to be around to protect them, or just to be there for them. It was at times like these that I needed to learn how to let go. God loved these young people much more than I did and, I could see that what really mattered was their relationship with him and, this was what we encouraged all the time. It is the same for all of us with our families. Knowing that God cares doesn't mean they will have an easy life, but it does mean that God will keep his promises to them just as he has for us.

Psalm 37:23-24 The Lord makes firm the steps of the one who delights in him; 24 though he may stumble, he will not fall for the Lord upholds him with his hand.

It is so very important that these children are given the opportunity to know their Heavenly Father for themselves.

6.4 Friendship

*28 And we know that in all things God works for the
good of those who love him, who have been
called according to his purpose.*
Romans 8:28 NIV

My final year had arrived and we were working to hard sort
out a system to continue to support the students. We were now
seeing some of them complete their studies and find work for
themselves. It was an exciting time. We were using as much of
the help given by the government, as we could to find places in
university or college. However, I would need to hand over the
visits to the home managers knowing that this would not be
easy for them. We refined the training sessions so that they
could have clear pattern for teaching the children leaving the
homes. The school was thriving and we now had a bus to
collect pupils from outlying areas.

I was asked to visit the States again, as my time with the
Charity was coming to an end, and I had a lovely time
celebrating my 70th birthday, on a farm in Wisconsin, although
I was sad not to be able to be with my own family. I visited
many of the sponsors and was able to give them up to date
information about the children they were supporting.

The Charity was about to celebrate 100 years of age, and
we decided to make it my farewell celebration too, which was
an ideal opportunity for a group of friends from my home
church to come out to Kenya. Most of them had been before so
they were keen also to revisit their own sponsor children and
work with the children in the home once again. It made my
leaving a great deal easier as they helped with managing the

volume of luggage. It was a great relief also to have company when I was feeling sad and saying goodbye to everyone.

When I began to write this account of my time in Kenya I chose the title, 'Never Too Old';' thinking particularly of the fact that I started this experience when I was 60. As the writing progressed, I realised it was much more about being Never Too Old to learn. We go through our lives with a lot of head knowledge about Christianity and don't put it to the test, because we think we can cope. I found myself constantly challenged, dealing with new situations and, learning how to turn to the Lord for answers. Did I really believe the promises God gives us in his Word? How do I take on board some of the things I knew in theory but never felt the need to put into practice?

I learned to trust that what God was saying is true. I learned how to talk with him as my Father, friend and comforter. When I was alone, I knew I was never alone, he filled my life with purpose and contentment. He showed me how to face problems and my favourite promise in times of difficulty was his promise to Jehoshaphat King of Judah, 2 Chronicles 20:15

'Do not be afraid or discouraged because of this vast army. For the battle is not yours, but God's.'

He gave me strength to face whatever happened and I felt very blessed.

The life we have been given is to bring glory to God himself. Just like he chose Israel to show the nations around them the greatness of God, we too should display that greatness through our lives. Our work was to help these children to know him and, alongside that, were all the other things we provided for them. God has plans for each one of us and, through those plans, he helps us to grow more like Jesus. He is faithful to us and we need to be faithful to him. The wonderful thing that he has been teaching me, recently, is that when we believe, and we are his, there is nothing that we can do that will separate us from him. He loves us no matter what.

It was hard leaving but, I managed to return 3 years later to see just how those young people were coping. I went with a friend who had often visited Kenya while I was there and we managed to trace about 63 of our former students, the joy of being with them again was great for everyone concerned. 62 of them were connected with their local church and some were serving among the youth or on the leadership teams. Some had made amazing progress in their chosen careers, an engineer, a doctor, school teachers, entrepreneurs. They looked out for each other too, and this turned into a lovely reunion for them. The school was thriving as well, with 360 children from the locality.

The Charity had started to train their staff for a reintegration programme. They joined with other Christian ministries who had devised a successful method of counselling and social care for the children found living on the streets. When Covid hit, the programme was accelerated because the Government wanted all the children in orphanages to be sent back to their wider families. This was very hard as the children had to be monitored to make sure that, they were safe and that, the families had enough food. The reintegration continues where both the children and their families are supported with counselling and physical care. Should the children have no family of their own, then foster families would be found.

The school continues to thrive and is still growing as they care for the children and their families in a very poor area. In fact, at the last count, it was over 500 children. The reputation of the school appears to be very good in the community and is also well respected in government circles.

The Lord has enriched my life beyond anything I could imagine.

- He has given me friends all over the world.

- He has answered my prayers in detail.

- He is caring for all the children I met.

- I am continuing in the new plans he has for me.

Looking back, I would wonder, "Why me?" but it was not about me it was about God himself.

This was His work! He could see that the children needed a "Mum" that they could talk to and he asked me to go. I had no idea of the work I would be asked to do but I know that if I had decided not to go, he would have sent someone else because he knew of the desperate needs of the children. This is the God whom we serve, he hears our cry and responds.

www.ingramcontent.com/pod-product-compliance
Lightning Source LLC
LaVergne TN
LVHW091257080426
835510LV00007B/293